Your Job Search Partner

A 10 Day, Step-by-Step, Opportunity Producing Job Search Guide

> *Don't Go Job Hunting Without Me!*

Your Job Search Partner

A 10 Day, Step-by-Step, Opportunity Producing Job Search Guide

CHERYL A. CAGE

Cage Consulting, Inc.

Career Consulting • Publishing

Your Job Search Partner
A 10 Day, Step-by-Step, Opportunity Producing, Job Search Guide

© 2002 by Cheryl A. Cage
Printed in the United States of America

Layout and Cover Design by Dan Miedaner
Published by Cage Consulting, Inc.

ISBN: 0-9714266-0-0
Library of Congress Control Number: 2002090199

Disclaimer: This book is sold with the understanding that the publisher and the author are not engaged in rendering legal, medical, or mental health services.

This book is a general information book on preparing for a job search. It is understood by the reader that the information contained in this book does not guarantee success. The author and publisher shall have neither liability nor responsibility to any person or entity with respect to any loss or damaged caused, or alleged to be caused directly or indirectly by the information contained in this book.

If you do not wish to be bound by the above, you may return this book to the publisher for a full refund.

Contents

Before We Begin

A Day

This book's definition of 'a Day' consists of a full eight hours of work.

If you have a full day to devote to a chapter and you begin at 8am, taking an hour or so for lunch, you should be completed with the section by 5PM.

If you must work in your spare time, simply expect to have a Day's work completed in about eight hours.

Searching for Your Career Niche?

It is extremely difficult to know how to search for a job, when you are not sure what you are searching for.

If you are undecided as to what type of work you want to pursue, or what type of company you want to pursue, I encourage you to take the time to do some career soul-searching.

Although this book is primarily a job search guide I have included a section on Skills Assessment in Appendix II. If you fit into either of the above categories I suggest that you turn to Appendix II and spend some time working through the Skills Assessment exercises *prior* to starting the 10 Day Job Search Plan. The clearer your job objectives are to you, the clearer the path to your goals.

Develop More Than One Area of Expertise

In today's uncertain job market it is becoming apparent you should have at least two marketable talents. With the cyclical nature of business, it is important to have a skill to 'fall back on' should your career field face lean times. No matter how dedicated you are to your career field, after you have completed the 10 Day Job Search Plan take some time and review the Skills Assessment Worksheet with the goal of uncovering a second hidden talent or area of interest.

Stories

The majority of the stories I share come from my own background. I did this because I want you to know that I have been in your shoes. I have personal experience in everything I write about. I've make mistakes, embarrassed myself, been dramatically confused, and had to apologize to numerous people—but I have learned from my mistakes and managed to find work that I love. So, basically, I suppose the reason I share so many of my own stories is to say, "Hey! If I can do it, so can you."

Your Job Search Partner

Allow Me to Introduce Myself

Since I am to be your partner in this job search endeavor and given the fact we will be spending the next ten days (or equivalent) together, and since you are *required* to share information about yourself with 'me' I feel it only fair to introduce myself a little more fully than a regular 'About the Author' paragraph.

As an Army Brat I chalked up attendance at ten different schools in Georgia, Maine, California, Kansas, Virginia, Alaska, and Panama. At a very early age I became comfortable meeting new people simply out of necessity. Every time we moved my mother would say, "You can't ride your bike until you find some kids your age." With this dire threat hanging over my head I became a pro at knocking on neighbor's doors and asking, "Ya got any kids my age?"

After graduating from college with a degree in psychology I became a flight attendant for Braniff International Airways (ever heard of it?). Braniff was first U.S. airline to declare bankruptcy. However, they were kind enough to stay in business long enough for me to fly around the world for free for five years, so I have no hard feelings.

After Braniff went bankrupt (leaving me stranded in London, but that's a story for another time) I went to work in sales and marketing for a national athletic club. Once again, five years seemed to be enough for me and I left that position to start my own company, Cage Consulting.

Initially I simply offered resume preparation. But, due to my airline connections, and the massive bankruptcies and layoffs that had occurred because of airline deregulation, I found myself receiving numerous requests for job search assistance from furloughed airline pilots. Consequently, since 1988 the majority of my clients have been pilots looking for help in preparing for airline pilot interviews. Cage Consulting offers paperwork assistance, videotaped mock interviews, and special concerns consulting.

Between 1990 and 1994 I worked as an Independent Consultant to the Air Line Pilots Association (ALPA—the national pilot union that represents over 60,000 professional airline pilots in the U.S.). In this role I presented my Job Search and Interview Preparation program to displaced airline pilots from PanAm, TWA, USAirways, and Aspen Airways, to name just a few.

I became a little weary of verbally delivering the same information to each and every new client, so in 1994 I wrote my first book *Checklist for Success: A Pilot's Guide to the Successful Airline Interview.* Cage Consulting has now published nine book titles, one CD, and one online training course. We strive to add two new titles to our publishing list every year.

Pilots, by nature, are methodical in their planning. My clients demanded from me a specific list of 'to-do' items that would help them prepare for their job search and allow them to shine during their airline interviews.

Because the advice I gave actually *helped* some of my clients get hired, many clients asked me to assist their non-pilot friends and relatives with various job search tasks. I quickly discovered that the proactive job search program that I had developed for my pilot clients worked extremely well for motivated individuals no matter what their field of interest. Thus, I sat down to write a complete job search guide that would include all the lessons I had learned since 1988. You are holding the final product in your hands.

When I married, some twenty-odd years ago, I was lucky enough to inherited two wonderful children, now grown and with children of their own. I share my house with an old dog, Andy, Benny the dachshund, and an African Grey parrot that talks. All . . . day . . . long. And sounds just like me.

My husband, Young, and I recently moved to Tucson, Arizona after spending 22 years in Denver, Colorado. It took me about a day and a half to realize I should have been living in the desert my whole life. Finally, I am warm.

OK, enough about me. Let's now focus on getting you the job you desire and deserve!

The Logic of the
10 Day Job Search Plan

Imagine yourself and a friend getting ready to take an adventure trip to a foreign country. Departure is in a month and you plan on being on the road for three weeks.

You call your friend and say, "OK! Let's start planning! Where do we want to go? Which flights should we book? What should we pack? What documents do we need? Do we need vaccinations or medications? How much money should we take? What sights do we *not* want to miss?"

Your friend replies, "Nahhh, there's no need to do any planning. Just pack a bunch of different clothes, bring a ton of money, and if we happen to pass something interesting we'll stop."

Hmmm, how successful will this trip be based on your friend's "wing it" method?

You forget to bring a raincoat and spend two miserable days because of the unexpected 48-hours of rain. (You did buy a cheap rain poncho that ripped after an hour. After that *no way* were you going to buy an expensive raincoat!) You wasted two days because you didn't have the required Visa to enter a particular country. You missed visiting the one museum you were desperate to see because you arrived on the one afternoon it was closed. All the charming little bargain hotels you were planning on frequenting were full and you ended up paying double for less desirable accommodations. Plus, your airline flights cost $200 more because you didn't book two weeks ahead of your travel date.

How different the trip would be if you took the time, at the beginning, to do some *basic* planning. You would have the right clothes, you would know the availability your favorite attractions, and you could book the cheapest airline flights. The entire trip would be tremendously more successful with less unexpected stresses because you spent a little bit of time planning at the onset.

A job search is no different. A bit of structured planning, at the beginning, can alleviate a great many unexpected surprises. Fewer surprises make the whole process a lot less stressful and, ultimately, a great deal more successful.

If you don't take the time to design a basic resume, which is easily personalized, you may well face many late nights writing a resume for an unexpected job interview your friend set up for you.

When a company representative calls, out-of-the-blue, to discuss the resume and cover letter you sent you stumble and mumble because you *just haven't had time* to research the company yet. Plus your copy of that resume and cover letter is not at your fingertips (it's on your desk somewhere, or perhaps in your bedroom?).

Your friend casually mentions his neighbor just hired a new sales person for her company. You would have been perfect for that job…but you didn't know she owned her own company!

When faced with having to search for a job many people feel completely overwhelmed. So, they "wing it." They read the want ads, search the Internet, and write a resume as opportunities arise. Then they are surprised because nothing happens.

It is easy to feel overwhelmed. There are so many things to do. Not to mention the fact a great deal of your comfort and happiness depends on your enjoyment of your work.

How do you conduct a successful job search? What are the *exact* tasks that need to be fulfilled? Once you know what those tasks are, how do you do them?

Where Do You Start?

You are not alone having these thoughts. Think for a moment, if you had the answers to the following questions *before* you began your job search, how much more confident and optimistic would you feel?

- How do I know that I'll be happy at this company?
- Does my paperwork adequately showcase my qualifications?
- Are my skills competitive?
- How am I going to get decision makers to speak with me?
- How should I react to the different personalities of various interviewers?
- What if I don't know the answer to a question?
- How can I prove that I am the right person for the job?
- How do I maintain my enthusiasm and stay motivated?
- How do I explain my problem areas?

Serious job seekers want to uncover all possible opportunities, but at the same time they don't want their job search to stretch on for months. Everyone wants to have the experience of being at the right place at the right time. When a job seeker chooses to accept employment he wants to feel as though it is just that: a choice. No one wants to settle for a job.

These are attainable goals! But, to reach these goals you can't "wing it"; you must have a logical plan. This is where I come in.

We are going to work together, you and I, as a team. I am the planner for our trip. I will outline the plan for your job search. You just fill in the blanks.

I have worked hard to remove the guesswork from your job search by breaking down the required tasks into a manageable, but action-packed, 10 Day Job Search Plan. Over the course of the next ten days (or equivalent) we will design, and then implement, a job search plan that will result in reaping more opportunities in less time.

> **We are going to work together, you and I, as a team, to make your job search a success.**

Over the course of the next 10 days *together* we will complete the following tasks:

- ◆ Learn the importance of your job search attitude.
- ◆ Critique your job search attitude.
- ◆ Organize your workspace.
- ◆ Discover, prioritize and develop your networking options.
- ◆ Become knowledgeable about the people involved in the hiring process.
- ◆ Discover and research your companies of interest.
- ◆ Determine both positive and negative experiences that best describe your skills and personality.
- ◆ Learn to discuss your experiences in a complete, yet concise manner.
- ◆ Design your entire paperwork presentation (resume, cover letters).
- ◆ Become aware of the most common interviewing mistakes.
- ◆ Prepare for your interviews.
- ◆ Assess your physical presentation.

These tasks are not difficult, but they can be time consuming. Please don't let impatience get in the way of completing every task. The work I am going to ask you to do each day is important and poor preparation in any of these areas can cost you time and money by making your job search longer. By the same token, if you are methodical in your preparation, the opportunities are endless.

If you are reading this book this means that your job situation has changed, or you want it to change.

The really terrific news is that with the strategies in this book, and with my help, you have taken the first step towards implementing positive change.

Your job search is an adventure. A great opportunity is out there, you just don't know exactly where it is! And, your future employer isn't privy to your home telephone number (yet).

It's up to us to get the word out about how lucky any employer would be to have you on their team. So, what are we waiting for? Let's get going.

Your Attitude

Morning: Critique
Afternoon: Cultivate

CHAPTER GOALS

- ◆ To understand the importance of attitude.
- ◆ To critique your present attitude.
- ◆ To develop and sustain a positive outlook.

Morning
Critique Your Current Attitude

When trouble strikes or when disappointment walks into your life you have a choice as to how you will react to your difficult circumstances.

Several years ago I was watching one of those news magazine programs. The story was about luck.

The man profiled in the program thought he was the unluckiest person in the world. You could feel his negativity dripping from every word he spoke. Though neatly dressed, he looked gray and unhealthy. He literally appeared to be stalked by a thundercloud.

On the other hand the woman profiled was convinced she had been born under a lucky star. You could tell the smile on her face was a permanent fixture. She seemed to sparkle.

The show's crew followed these two people around for one day. The man forgot his umbrella, ruined his good shoes and was very upset. The woman also left her umbrella, her hair became drenched but she thought it was great because it added curl to her hairdo. The man went to a job interview and it didn't go well. The woman landed a new contract.

Talk about self-fulfilling prophecies.

Now, I know this is a simplistic tale. But the clear, however unscientific, message of the story was: Attitude contributes a great deal to how our lives play out. This message parallels my personal experience.

Having worked with over 4,000 job applicants one of my initial criteria for gauging a person's chances for success is: Do they have a positive attitude?

We can plan and implement the most technically perfect job search in the world, but if you deliver your message with a less-than-positive attitude the results will be disappointing. No matter how talented an individual, no one relishes working with a negative, sad sack personality.

> ## Attitude can be your ally *or* your enemy!

A positive attitude is such a vital ingredient for success I've allotted one whole day for you to dissect your current attitude and to learn how to make your attitude consistently upbeat. Spending eight hours may seem like a lot. However, because "your attitude really *does* determine your altitude" your attitude can be your biggest strength, or your greatest downfall.

There may be many reasons for your current employment situation. Perhaps you lost a job due to company layoff, or you were in line for a promotion that disappeared with the bankruptcy of your company. You might just be starting out and struggling with finding that first professional position. Or, perhaps you were terminated because of your individual job performance.

No matter what your circumstances you may feel as though your luck has turned sour.

Nonsense. Downturns, both personal and professional, are a fact of life. Every single person in the world (no matter how successful they appear) has had their share of trials and tribulations. We all have troubles. But, we also all have a choice as to how we approach our troubles.

Several years ago a friend of mine, Audrey, received some very bad news. She was scared and feeling as though her world was about ready to crumble. But, she is a private person and chose not to share the news with anyone but a few very close friends.

Audrey had planned a luncheon for several coworkers to take a tour through her new house and it was to take place the day after she received the bad news. Being a person who refuses to let life's problems play havoc with her daily schedule, she did not cancel the luncheon. I happened to arrive at the same time as a young coworker, Barb. Barb had an aura about her that said, "Watch out! Tragedy is just around the corner."

As Barb took off her coat she said to Audrey, "You know I was just walking up your driveway and thinking about how lucky you are. You have a great job, a great husband, this new house. Plus, you get to travel a lot." She looked at Audrey and said, "You don't have any problems do you?" This young woman was completely serious, and completely oblivious. She honestly believed that because someone was regularly upbeat and positive it must be because they had no worries! Oh, how wrong she was!

Attitude can be your ally or your enemy. All the hard work I've put into designing your 10 Day Job Search Plan will not work if your attitude is sour, depressed, and negative. Now is the time to be totally honest with yourself. It's time for an attitude 'gut check'! Remember, we are the only two here.

There are a few important questions I'd like you to ponder. So, make yourself comfortable . . . get another cup of coffee if you have to. I'll wait.

> **You control how you react to difficult situations.**

As you review the following questions be on the lookout for thought processes that are causing you to feel helpless, negative, and subsequently unproductive. Write down any negative behaviors you discover.

Comfy? No distractions? Ready to truly be honest with yourself? Good, let's go!

The Questions and Your Answer Worksheet

For this worksheet I provide *The Questions* and you provide *Your Answer*. To help you understand what type of answers you are searching for I also provide you with questions to *Ask Yourself* to help you discover your answers.

1. *The Question:* **What are my first thoughts upon waking in the morning?**

   Ask Yourself: Are my initial thoughts positive? Do I feel energized and ready-to-go? Or are my thoughts primarily negative? Do I feel more like pulling the covers over my head, or simply reading the paper all morning?

   Your Answer:

2. *The Question:* **How do I react to my loved ones?**

   Ask Yourself: Am I patient and attentive? Or do I snap and feel intruded upon?

   Your Answer:

3. *The Question:* **How do I react to advice given to me by friends and family?**

   Ask Yourself: Do I listen carefully to others thoughts? Do I take time to digest comments and advice? Or do I automatically feel myself becoming defensive when anyone gives me advice?

   Your Answer:

Your Job Search Partner ©2002 Cage Publishing, Tucson, Arizona

4. *The Question:* **What type of conversations do I have with people?**

   Ask Yourself: Is the majority of my time spent talking about negative topics (loss of a job, illness, unfairness in the world, etc.)? Or do I take the time to "smell the roses" and think about how many areas of my life are happy?

   Your Answer:

5. *The Question:* **How do I react to strangers?**

   Ask Yourself: Do I smile? Do I view people as basically good? Or do I have the feeling everyone else in the world has better luck than I?

   Your Answer:

6. *The Question:* **How do I spend my day?**

   Ask Yourself: Am I thinking creatively about what is needed to move forward in order to reach my goals? Or am I just going through the motions of pursuing change?

   Your Answer:

Search for Reasons Worksheet

OK, now that you have answered six basic questions it is time to search for the reasons behind any unproductive behaviors you unmasked. You must ask yourself: What is happening inside of me, or around me, that is contributing to my unproductive behaviors?

> You must be honest with yourself if you desire true positive change.

The point of me asking you these questions is NOT to make you feel bad, it is to help you root out unproductive behaviors (and we all have them . . . even me). Until you can clearly see that a behavior is negatively impacting your life it is impossible to begin to initiate positive change. You've taken the first step towards positive change by providing yourself with honest answers to some important questions. Now we need to uncover the REASONS for your unproductive behavior.

To explain what you need to be searching for, let me give you some examples of common Possible Reasons for unproductive behavior.

Examples Only

The Question: **How do I react to my loved ones?**

Your Answer: I snap at people all the time.

Possible Reasons: I seem to be spending a lot of my day asking myself, "Why did this happen to me (getting laid off, terminated, downsized, etc.)?" instead of, "How can I change my circumstances?"

Or, I feel angry that my friends aren't going through the same thing. I feel guilty about being angry.

The Question: **How do I spend my day?**

Your Answer: I can't seem to focus on any task for longer than a few minutes.

Possible Reasons: My lack of focus and motivation could be a result of spending too much time with Chris (former coworker, friend, relative). He is so negative and angry. I seem to be catching a negative attitude and I need to limit my time with him.

Or, I am so worried about finances that when I sit down to do job search tasks I end up worrying about money that is leaving my bank account, but thinking nothing about how I could be putting money in my bank account.

The Question: **How do I react to advice given to me by others?**

Your Answer: I automatically become defensive.

Possible Reasons: I feel as though they don't know what I am going through . . . they have a job! Realistically, they have some good ideas but when I take advice I feel like more of a failure because I can't figure this out myself.

Now it's your turn. Simply list your initial *Answers* for the first six *Questions,* and then add on *Possible Reasons* for your behavior.

You should be extremely proud of yourself if you are able to discover new insights into your behavior.

Search for Reasons Worksheet

1. **What are my first thoughts upon waking in the morning?**

   Your Answer: (remember, just list what you listed in the previous Worksheet)

   Possible Reasons:

2. **How do I reacting to my loved ones?**

   Your Answer:

   Possible Reasons:

3. **How do I react to advice given to me by friends and family?**

   Your Answer:

   Possible Reasons:

4. **What type of conversations do I have with people?**

    Your Answer:

    Possible Reasons:

5. **How do I react to strangers?**

    Your Answer:

    Possible Reasons:

6. **How am I spending my day?**

    Your Answer:

    Possible Reasons:

You may well have some additional difficult questions you would like to try to answer. The worksheet on the following page offers some common situations that, perhaps, you are facing in your own life right now. Remember, the only person who can truthfully answer these questions is you.

Additional Questions Worksheet

- Why am I irritated with my spouse so often?
- Why am I so cranky with my children?
- Why am I not exercising?
- Why do I not feel like socializing?
- Why am I avoiding my friends?
- Why am I going shopping when I have no money coming in?
- Why am I keeping myself busy with household chores instead of tackling my job search?
- Why did I get fired?
- Why am I not able to find work I love?

You may want to answer some of the questions I've listed above, or you may have different ones you want to investigate.

7. **Question:**

   Your Answer:

   Possible Reasons:

8. **Question:**

   Your Answer:

   Possible Reasons:

9. **Question:**

   Your Answer:

   Possible Reasons:

10. **Question:**

    Your Answer:

    Possible Reasons:

Your Job Search Partner ©2002 Cage Publishing, Tucson, Arizona

Afternoon
Cultivating an Upbeat Attitude

If you have come to the realization that your attitude could use some adjustment: Good for you! You have taken the first step towards instituting positive change.

If you discover you are fairly satisfied that your attitude is primarily positive: Good for you! Celebrate your outlook and strive to maintain it at all costs.

No matter which group you belong to there is always more to learn. Towards this goal I'd like to introduce to you Five Successful Person Traits that seem to be evident in people who survive, and even thrive, in good times and bad.

> Over the next ten days work hard to incorporate the Five Successful Person Traits into your daily life.

Over the next ten days work hard to incorporate the Five Successful Person Traits into your daily life. A positive attitude IS something that you can teach yourself.

The Five Successful Person Traits
Trait #1

Successful people have the ability to recognize when change is needed and a desire to discover and implement steps that will result in positive change. These people not only have an ability to take an honest look at themselves, but they are also open to constructive critique from others.

Trait #2

Successful people remove damaging, negative statements from their thinking and replace those thoughts with proactive approaches. Do not misunderstand; these people are not "Pollyannas." They are not simply walking around thinking happy thoughts and ignoring reality. Successful people are realists with positive attitudes.

- ◆ They don't think: I can't do it.
  They think: I can do anything if I put my mind to it.

- ◆ They don't think: That's a stupid idea.
  They think: This is an unusual, but interesting, idea.

- ◆ They don't think: I'm not good enough at math/English/ computers/sales, etc. to do that type of work.
  They think: I need to update my skills. How can I do that?

- They don't think: I can't do anything about it.
  They think: Yes, I have a problem. What steps do I need to take to solve it?

Trait #3

Successful people do not allow their egos to get in the way of positive change.

If you were to chat with a person you view as successful most likely you would learn that at some time during their life they faced career problems. Perhaps because of economic downturns or company layoff they took a job that was lower in pay and professional standing in order to fulfill their financial obligations.

- An airline pilot was furloughed on a Tuesday and on Thursday started his own handyman service.
- A banker was laid off from his management job and took an interim job working for his dentist as a receptionist.
- An entrepreneur quit his job to start his own business. The business failed and he asked to have his old job back.

Successful people survive, and thrive, because they don't allow ego to get in the way of doing what is necessary to get back on their feet.

Trait #4

Successful people seek out others with the same positive approach towards life.

It is rare to meet a truly successful person who is surrounded by negative people. Successful people take the time to identify people in their lives who suck the energy and enthusiasm out of them. They then lessen the amount of time they spend with these people.

Successful people strive to spend more time with individuals who possess an overall positive outlook.

Trait #5

Successful people don't require immediate gratification. They are willing to 'pay their dues.'

The majority of successful people had to work long and hard to reach their goals. Their success didn't happen overnight.

- A woman with a successful horse boarding business worked for over five years before reaching financial stability. True financial success took much longer. The only horse boarding facility she could initially afford was located miles outside city limits. Customers were few and far between. But, she knew the city would grow and, as it did, more people would be living closer to her stable. Until the stable could begin to pay for itself she did odd jobs to keep her business going. Because she was able to wait to reach her ultimate goal she is now able to live the life she envisioned for so many years.

More Examples

I want to own my own business.

Immediate Gratification Trait: I don't want to have to work full-time and then have to give up my weekends and evenings for two years.

Successful Person Trait: If I work on the weekends and in the evenings on my business in two years I should be able to quit my job and work my business full-time. If I start today, in two years I will be working at my new company instead of getting ready for my daily commute.

I want to write a book.

Immediate Gratification Trait: I don't want to have to work full-time and then have to give up my weekends and evenings for two years for something that probably won't ever get published.

Successful Person Trait: If I budget ten hours a week (early in the morning before work, or late at night when the kids are asleep) I could finish in about ten months. That means I could send it to a publisher in less than a year! It would be exciting just to actually say I wrote a book, even if it never gets published.

You need to remove the desire for instant gratification. Develop an ability to obtain gratification from the fact that you have a plan to reach your goal.

Roadblocks and Roadblock Busters

Now that you have spent some time reviewing your current attitude, and have made the decision to incorporate the Five Successful Person Traits into your daily life, let's review some common positive attitude roadblocks. Once we acknowledge these roadblocks I will then share with you some simple steps to help you bust through these roadblocks and maintain your new positiveness.

Positive Attitude Roadblocks
Inappropriate Pride

One of the most difficult situations to face when implementing a job search is not having a job. Whether you were laid off or terminated you most likely are facing two problems: feelings of self-doubt and financial concerns.

Don't allow your pride to stand in the way of reaching your goals.

It takes a tremendous amount of energy to worry. It is not surprising that someone who is worried and sad usually has a low energy level. Low energy means less ability to be creative, enthusiastic, and focused—all necessary ingredients for a short, successful job search. It can be a vicious cycle.

So, first, let's prioritize the problems brought on by being without work: self-doubt and financial concerns. Which of these two problems would be the quickest to solve?

Obviously, if you could take care of your financial obligations (either in full or in part) so that you weren't completely dependent on savings or whatever financial aids you might be receiving (unemployment, etc.) your stress level could be much lower.

Look back at Successful Person Trait #3.

Now, more than ever, your outlook on life is going to impact the success you have in your job search.

If you need to get a part-time job to make ends meet, do it! Don't let your pride get in the way of getting back on solid financial footing.

> *One day I was an international flight attendant with big plans to move into management. The next day my airline went bankrupt and I was an unemployed ex-flight attendant with a house payment, insurance payment, car payment—and no job. To top if off my last paycheck bounced. Desperately needing an income, I turned to waiting tables.*

> *It took me four days, but I was finally offered a waitress position at a popular local restaurant. On my first day I was told that before I could even begin waiting tables I had to bus tables for two weeks! Aggghhh! Now I was really miserable. But, I had no choice. I swallowed my pride and bussed the tables.*

It was one of the best decisions I ever made.

Although it was a job I didn't enjoy, it did alleviate my biggest immediate concern—money. I told myself every day when I counted my tips, "At least I can pay my bills."

In hindsight, I am especially proud that I didn't "throw in the apron" when things got tough. I was proactive in dealing with my difficult circumstances. I also learned the very comforting lesson that, no matter what, I will always find a way to survive.

You may well find yourself faced with circumstances where your ego stands up and says, "No way. You don't want to do that, it's too embarrassing!" You can do anything for a short period of time. Don't allow your pride to stand in the way of reaching your goals. You still have a great deal of control over your life; with hard work, tenacity and the ability to control your ego—*you will be successful!*

Joyless Employment.

Another common situation is to be working at a job you do not enjoy. It is not uncommon for people facing this situation to also have very low energy levels. Being unfulfilled and misdirected can really sap your energy. Low energy means less ability to be creative, enthusiastic, and focused—once again, all necessary ingredients for a successful job search. If you find yourself in this predicament, it is probably unrealistic to try to love your current job. However, it is realistic to change the way you *view* your job.

You must begin to view your current job simply as a tool that is going to help you to reach a happier life. This job is helping you to meet your financial responsibilities. Use your current situation as a motivation tool to push you towards finding a job that is more suitable. Refocus the energy you are using to dislike your current position and use it to invigorate your job search.

> When I began Cage Consulting I had no money to fund the business. That meant I had to find a second job while building my company.
>
> I searched for a situation that would allow me to set my own hours and found a position with a national jewelry company. My job was to visit twelve stores, in an eighty mile radius, once a month and do complete inventory of every single earring, bracelet, necklace, ring and hair ornament in stock. Need I really take up space describing my dislike of this job?
>
> I was able to stick it out because I viewed the job as a tool. Every time I sat in the storeroom surrounded by 200 single earrings that required me to play matchmaker, I would say to myself, "Every earring I touch brings me one step closer to being able to own my own business."

No matter how you may be feeling right now, I am here to tell you, you have a great deal of control over your life. The job you are in now does not have to be the end of the road! If you want to change your life, then get on the stick and start doing the work that will result in change.

Yes, it will take lots of hard work. Yes, you probably will give up your time off evenings, weekends, and holidays. Perhaps you won't be able to take a family vacation this year because of the need to save money.

But, each morning take a moment to take a long-term view of what your life could be like a year or two down the road. Won't all this hard work be worth it to be able to wake up in the morning and feel excited about going to work?

Shyness

Shyness can feel like a huge anchor tied around your neck during a job search. I know, and have worked with, many people who struggle with shyness. Even those of us who are lucky enough to not suffer from shyness have experienced its' pain.

> *When I was in college I attended a formal military party with my parents. The room was filled with military officers in dress uniform and women in beautiful gowns. I was extremely nervous. My father introduced me to a group of about eight military officers and their spouses and one of the officers said, "So, Cheryl, where do you go to school?"*
>
> *I couldn't remember. Thank heavens my Dad did.*

Remind yourself on a daily basis (and take comfort in the fact) that every single person in the world has experienced heart palpitations and brain freezes in social and professional settings.

Another fear felt by shy people is the fear of embarrassing yourself in front of others.

> *During the first week of Flight Attendant Training we were introduced to cabin service through conducting a complete first class meal service in the airplane mockup. I was assigned the task of removing 'passengers' (actually my classmates) food trays and storing them in the galley. This was serious business to everyone in the room (especially since two of our classmates had already been terminated because of mistakes).*

As I cleared the trays I couldn't figure out where I was supposed to put all the leftover food. Well, at home you scraped the plates and put it in the garbage right? So, that's what I did. Until I scraped the second plate and realized the garbage can was already full. This can't be right, I thought.

At that exact moment the Instructor also realized it wasn't right. She decided to use me as an example of how NOT to do a meal service. "For heavens sake Cheryl" she said, "you aren't working in a cafeteria! Put the entire tray in the galley container and the caterers will remove the entire package." I felt like an idiot, but I survived. And, believe me it wasn't the last stupid mistake I made.

Stop anyone (and I mean anyone, an actor, politician, successful businessperson) on the street and ask them to tell you about an embarrassing situation where they were the star. I guarantee that within 30 seconds they will have thought of at least three! And, they survived, and even thrived, didn't they?

Chronic shyness can be a tremendous roadblock to reaching your goals: if you let it! The good news is that if you can make yourself take a *few simple steps* to face your shyness the accomplishment of taking action will give you added confidence.

> **Plan for conversations in advance.**

I know it is not possible to wake up one morning and say, "Ok, as of today I'm no longer shy." However, it is possible for you to not allow your shyness to dominate you. Like any other problem the sooner you admit shyness is inhibiting your progress, and the sooner you take a few steps towards controlling your shyness, the less your shyness will be a factor in your job search.

A common theme among shy people is, "When I meet new people I can't think of anything to say." Fair enough. Then let's assume this is going to happen. How can you untie your tongue and get your brain working?

By planning your conversations in advance.

Start by committing to memory a list of generic questions you can ask whenever you feel the conversation is waning or when you would like to detract attention from yourself.

Keep your questions focused on general areas and away from specific controversial subjects (Do you attend church? What are your political leanings? Why are you wearing that horrible toupee?).

You may use the following questions in any professional or social setting.

- What type of work do you do?
- How long have you been in your current job?
- What do you like most about your work?
- What is the outlook for growth in your career field?
- What is the most difficult situation you have ever encountered in your work?
- Have you always lived in this area?
- You just came back from vacation? Where did you go?
- How did you become involved in this group?
- How did you meet our hosts?
- I'm not from this part of town. Are there some good restaurants in this area?

Another way to keep your brain working is to read: newspapers, books, and magazines. When you are going to be attending a gathering look for interesting articles that you can share, or general situations you can use for discussion (but always remembering to stay away from controversial subjects with new people.)

- Did you happen to read the article about the group of CEO's that are looking for new energy ideas in which to invest?
- I just read an interesting article about Lewis and Clark. Did you know that only one man was lost during their two-year exploration? And he died of a ruptured appendix. Do you enjoy historical books?
- I just re-read *The Grapes of Wrath*. Have you read it? (If not ask another question) What types of books do you enjoy?
- I heard you say you had children. Did you happen to read the article about classroom size in today's paper? Do you feel your children's classrooms are too crowded? How do you like the schools in this area?
- I just saw a great movie. Have you seen it? (If not, ask another question.) What type of movies do you enjoy? What is your all-time favorite movie?

If you find yourself really uncomfortable, remember, most people LOVE to talk about themselves. If you need some time to gather your thoughts, ask a question that requires a lengthier response.

- How did you get started in your career?
- Tell me about your company.
- What has been the best vacation you have ever taken?
- Tell me about your children.

Don't be too hard on yourself. Shyness is a personality trait that is tough to overcome, but remember it is only ONE trait you possess. Take time to give yourself a pat on the back for all the positive personal traits you possess.

Now that you are aware of some common roadblocks it is time to ask yourself: What personal roadblocks am I facing?

1. _____

2. _____

3. _____

Now let's take a look at some proactive ways to help yourself break through whatever roadblocks you may be facing.

Positive Attitude Roadblock *Busters*
Join a Job Search and/or a
Displaced Workers Support Group

It is important to know you are not alone. Meeting on a regular basis with people who share your situation will allow you to realize that you are not the only one having feelings of frustration and doubt.

However, be careful. Join groups that are upbeat and proactive. The last thing you need is to get bogged down by "woe is me" stories. You want to leave each meeting with fresh ideas and renewed energy.

If you can't find a group in your area, start one on your own. During the airline bankruptcies in the late 80s and early 90s many of the displaced pilots organized local Family Awareness Groups. Pilots and their families got together on a regular basis to have dinner and to talk about their situation. These groups developed into wonderful, sustained support systems and life-long friends were made.

There may be other professionals from all different fields in your town who are facing the same situation. Take the initiative and invite them to your home for a potluck dinner. Network together. You most likely will discover that you have diverse skills and are looking for different types of jobs. During the gathering have each person take a turn to discuss what type of job he or she is looking for. Someone might have an "in" at a computer firm you have interest in, but he is interested in a financial planning position.

Also, don't forget that your family members may be facing their own worries and doubts. Talk openly about your concerns. It will make it much easier to survive, and thrive, if you have a good support system.

Give Yourself Pep Talks.

Realize that the harder and smarter you work on your job search, the quicker you will be able to change your circumstances. Say to yourself, "If I get these resumes out, make these phone calls, or go to this networking group *today*, the chances are much greater I will find the lead I need to find my interesting job."

Also remember that it is OK to feel awful—once in awhile. If you are feeling totally discouraged treat yourself to a movie, a long afternoon walk, a good book, or a nice meal. But don't allow yourself to wallow for more than a brief afternoon. If you are having a particularly bad day, don't let yourself completely off the hook. Even on your worst day you must work at least for one hour on your job search. Send out at least two resumes and make at least four phone calls.

This job search is a treasure hunt. A good job is out there—you just don't know where it is. And your potential employer certainly won't magically get your name and address. The only way people will know about you is for you to get out in the world and tell them about yourself.

Unemployed?—Procrastination Is Your Enemy!

Set the alarm clock. Get up in the morning and shower and dress as though you are going to work. Because you are going to work . . . you are working on your job search.

Understand clearly that unless your uncle owns the company you want to work for or your mom is the former Secretary of State with contacts all over the world, getting an interview and landing a job takes creativity, dedication, and planning. The majority of people must make their own opportunities. They must get up in the morning with a plan, spend the day executing that plan, and the evening critiquing how well, or poorly, the plan is working.

If you don't send out that resume today, if you don't make that call today—someone else will and that someone might land the job that would be perfect for you.

View Every Encounter as An Opportunity.

When I don't feel like going to a marketing meeting, business appointment, or a networking meeting I make myself go. I am usually rewarded. I meet someone interesting or learn something new (sometimes it is just that the refreshments are really good, like chocolate layer cake!). You must approach each meeting with the attitude of, "I wonder what I'll learn here." View every meeting or networking group as an opportunity.

Make a Final Decision Only with All the Information.

Do not allow yourself to assume: "They aren't going to hire this year," "I don't have the experience they are looking for,' or "I'm not sure I want to work for them." These types of statements are assumptions, not facts.

You do not have to make a decision until someone says, "Can you start Monday?" In business things can change overnight. On Tuesday the company wasn't hiring, Wednesday, they received an unexpected foreign contract, and by Friday they hired ten new employees.

Apply everywhere that presents an opportunity you find interesting. Go to every offered interview. Only in this way can you make an informed decision.

Learn From, But Also Be Able to Laugh at, Your Mistakes.

It was 8:00 AM and I was waiting for a client. This particular client had worked very hard to schedule an appointment with me and, consequently, was making a special trip to our office from out of state. I had not spoken to this client and had not taken the time to review his file the night before.

A very young man walked in the door. I assumed this was my client. We began our appointment a little early. At about 9:15 one of my staff interrupted me (which is extremely unusual because we try never to interrupt a session).

It turns out I was working with the wrong client. But because we were over an hour into our session it was impossible to switch clients.

Because I had neglected to review paperwork the night before I looked extremely unprofessional in front of my clients and my staff—not to mention I lost a great deal of money since I didn't charge either client.

Even though it was an embarrassing and uncomfortable day, eventually I was able to laugh at my stupidity. But, I also learned an important lesson: review paperwork the night before! (Fortunately, my original client was very understanding and accepted having a chance to talk with me for an hour after his session.)

Ask for Help If You Need It!

I am a firm believer in doing things yourself. However, I am also a firm believer in asking for help if you need it.

As you proceed through your job search and interviews, you may find some areas where you need polish. Perhaps you are stalled in making a career choice, or maybe you are not interviewing to your full potential.

Then, perhaps, it is the time to go to an outside professional for help.

◆ When looking for professional assistance choose a company that offers a menu of services. I feel strongly about choosing an hourly fee service, instead of an up-front fee. Select a company that offers a menu of services such as: resume services, interview preparation, and skills assessment.

But, remember your job search is your personal responsibility and, ultimately, the outcome is in your hands.

Chapter Summary

❑ Your have control over your attitude.

❑ The key to change is to be honest with yourself about your strengths and weaknesses.

❑ Work hard to incorporating the Five Successful Person Traits.

❑ Don't let pride get in your way of financial stability.

❑ Don't let your shyness get in the way of opportunity.

❑ A positive attitude can make your entire job search more productive and enjoyable.

Get Organized

CHAPTER GOALS

- ◆ To organize your workspace.
- ◆ To begin developing Opportunity Lists and networking opportunities.

One of my major goals is to help make your job search more organized. Nowhere is disorganization more prevalent than in the workspace and the daily plan.

First let's organize your workspace. I have listed everything you will need at your job search desk.

Work Space

Select an area for your job search desk. You want it in a private area of your home near a telephone and your computer. (You may receive unexpected phone calls from potential employers and you will want to be able to get your hands on their informational files quickly.)

Your workspace should be supplied with:

❑ A phone with voice mail. Have a professional message on voice mail. No singing, no jokes and no children making your announcements.

❑ File Folders (for Tracking Information).

❑ Wall calendar with appointments listed so you can easily glance at your availability for interviews, etc.

❑ Business size envelopes for letters, and manila folders (to mail resumes or job applications without folding).

❑ Return address stamp or labels. (Your return address should list your name only.)

❑ Stamps. Buy enough stamps so that you don't have to stop working to replenish your supply.

❑ Letterhead. You can design your letterhead on your computer; it does not (in fact should not) be fancy. Simply list your name, address, phone numbers, and email address on the top of the paper.

Cheryl A. Cage
1236 West Cayton Canyon Loop
Tucson, Arizona 85773
(Home) 520-555-1212, (Cell) 520-555-1234
cheryl@cageconsulting.com

❑ Business cards. These simple cards should list your name, address, phone numbers and email address. You may do these on your computer, or go to a copy center and have them done. Simple white or ivory colored cards will do. No need to spend a lot of money.

❑ The following items will be stored near your desk. (Today's goal is to just be aware of the periodicals/Internet addresses you will need. However, we will not be doing in-depth research until Day Five.)

• You need daily access to appropriate local newspapers (through delivery or the Internet).

• If you are open to relocating investigate the best local paper in your geographical areas of interest. Many of these papers now have online sites, so you don't have to spend money for a subscription.

• Subscriptions to trade and professional journals. (More on Day Five and in Appendix I.)

Tracking Information Files

Make a separate file for each company you contact, or that contacts you. In this file keep:

❑ Company research (articles, company reports, notes from interviews with employees).

❑ Copies of documents you sent to the company (cover letters, resumes, follow-up letters).

❑ Copies of all documents you receive from the company (invitations to interview, etc.).

Perhaps you store information on your computer. This works well for paperwork you send *out*. However do not neglect to track correspondence you *receive* from potential employers.

Tracking Information File

Position Pursuing: _____

Company Name: _____

Address: _____

Main Phone Number: _____

Main Fax Number: _____

Main Website Address: _____

Specific Company Contacts

Name: _____

Position: _____

How I met this person: _____

Phone Number: _____

Fax Number: _____

Email: _____

Information/Comments

List information sent and received. Take good notes every time you speak to someone, mail or email something, or receive correspondence.

_____

_____

_____

_____

_____

_____

_____

_____

_____

_____

_____

_____

_____

_____

_____

Opportunity Lists

You have your workspace organized, tracking files at the ready. But, wait! You don't have rich and famous friends or relatives who can tell you where the opportunities are, or the intimate details of a company's future plans? So how do you discover your own opportunities? Where are you going to find your companies of interest?

Have you ever had the experience of watching TV, or reading a newspaper, and an unusual city name or company name catches your attention? Then, over the course of the next several days, you are amazed at the number of times you hear this name. This happens simply because your initial interest planted the seed of noticing that particular name. It is not that the name is mysteriously now popping up everywhere you look, you are simply noticing it more often.

The same approach works with a job search. The more people that know *specifically* what type of job you are pursuing, the more 'eyes and ears' you will have working on your behalf. This premise is the reason for making Opportunity Lists.

Get yourself a cup of coffee and a pad of paper. Sit in your favorite thinking spot. The first step towards finding a job is getting the word out.

You are going to be personally contacting all of the people on these lists. Don't worry, in Day Seven I will help you write your letters. For now just focus on making each list as complete as possible.

After you complete your initial lists show them to your spouse or trusted friend and ask for any additional suggestions for contacts they may have.

Opportunity List A
Friends and Relatives

The people on this list are the people that know you and love you (or at least like you).

- List every friend and every relative (near and distant). Don't leave anyone out!
- Research complete names, titles (Dr., Colonel, etc.)
- Gather correct addresses, phone numbers and email addresses.
- List the person's occupation.
- List industries you believe this person may have insight into.
- Leave extra space under the industries to list what type of letter you will be writing (more about letter writing in upcoming chapters.)

Tracking File (Example)

Name .... Captain Bill Friend
Address/phone .... 123 Denver Place
                                       Tucson, Arizona 85733
                                       Home: 555-121-5555
                                       Cell: 555-121-5556
                                       Billjones@computer.net
Profession .... Airline pilot for ABC Airlines.
Fields .... Aviation, aerospace, engineering companies.
Letter/Date Sent .... Friend letter/ 10-3-02

- You should have at least seven names on your initial list.

Opportunity List B
Business Acquaintances

These are people you may know only slightly.

- Obviously it is easy to list people involved directly in your industry, but don't short change yourself by leaving people off your list who seem to be 'long shots' in knowing someone who could help you. Perhaps a former client comes from an engineer background and you are pursuing a position within engineer parts sales. Maybe your child's teacher's husband is in law enforcement and you are looking for information on pursuing a Police Officer position. Have a degree in biology or related sciences? Your family doctor may be able to offer names of the pharmaceutical salespeople he deals with.
- Research complete names, titles (such as Dr., Colonel, etc.).
- Gather correct addresses, phone numbers and email addresses.
- Remember these are names of people who DO NOT necessarily have to be involved in your particular field.

Tracking File (Example)

Perhaps you are searching for a position in Information Technology.

Name .... Dr. Bob Acquaint
Address/Phone .... 4478 Network Way
Tucson, Arizona 85777
555-123-3456
bob@acquaint.net
Profession .... Orthodontist
How Known .... Son's orthodontist
Fields .... He is member of the Chamber of Commerce, perhaps he knows someone in the computer industry or someone who needs IT assistance? Also possible leads within Pharmaceutical sales company who may need IT assistance.
Letter/Date Sent .... Business Acquaintance/10-06-02

- You should have ten names on your initial list.

Opportunity List C
Contacts for Informational Interviewing

This list will contain names of businesses or companies where you feel you could make a contribution, but they are not currently hiring. You may not personally know anyone on this list. You will be contacting these people to request an Informational Interview.

After the bankruptcy of Braniff Airways I was at a complete loss. Although I knew I didn't want to return to being a flight attendant, I was confused as to what I really wanted to do, or even what skills I had.

One day I took myself out for coffee and made a dream list. I listed what I envisioned my ideal workday to be. My list included being in an atmosphere where I would be interacting with different people throughout the day. I wanted to be responsible for my own time management, and I thought I might have some fairly marketable skills in writing and wanted to use those skills to help design promotional materials.

Then I asked myself, "What business looks interesting to me?" The athletic club industry was first on my list. In the early 80s this was a fairly new field that offered many social aspects, lots of different people to meet, and varied work schedules—plus there were many new clubs opening within my city. Armed with this new self-knowledge, I did some research and came up with the names of four athletic clubs in my area.

I wrote a letter to each of the club directors, describing my background and interests. I ended the letter by asking for an appointment to meet with the director in person. The focus of my letter was: I am just gathering information on my options.

Three days later the director of the largest, most progressive club called me. He was putting together a new sales and marketing department and invited me to come in and talk with him based strictly on the letter I had written.

Although I had no sales or marketing experience, I felt extremely comfortable discussing my interests because I had spent so much time determining my strengths and goals. This approach paid off. I was hired for the new department and worked for this company for over five years.

- Prioritize the companies and industries in order of desirability. (Don't try new letters or ideas on your most promising companies. Make sure you like your resume and cover letters before sending out information to your most coveted prospects.)
- Identify, by name, the person in the company or within the industry who is at least one level up from the position you would be pursuing. For example, if you think you could find a niche in computer sales, your target person might be the Computer Sales Manager.
- Remember, these are people who are involved, in some way, in the type of work you are pursuing.
- You should have a minimum of fifteen names on your initial list.

Opportunity List C *(continued)*
Contacts for Informational Interviewing

Tracking File (Example)

Perhaps you are looking for a position as an Office Manager for a medical business.

Name .... Dr. Susan Bennett
Address/Phone .... 1212 Brown Lane
                                         Tucson, AZ 88888
                                         (555) 212-3923
                                         drbennett@computer.com
Profession .... Dermatologist Associates
How Known .... Saw an ad about a talk she is giving, she may need to expand
                                         her business?
Fields .... Medical Administration
Letter/Date Sent .... Information Interviewing/ 10-03-02

Opportunity List D
Companies Actively Hiring

This list is pretty straightforward. It will be comprised of your companies of interest that are actively hiring.

◆ Remember, I'll be helping you to write your letters. Right now, just focus on listing as many companies as you can.

Tracking File (Example)

Name of Company .... Cage Consulting
Contact Person .... Bob Smith
Address/phone .... 4545 Forth Ave
                                                    Tucson, Arizona 55555
                                                    (555) 343-3434
                                                    smith@consult.com
Where heard about job .... Tucson Daily News
Letter/Date Sent .... Cover letter/10/502

◆ You should have at least 6 companies on this initial list.

OK. Now that you have the minimum number of names suggested for each list keep the lists handy in order to add names or companies. However, we won't be working on introductory letters to these people for several days.

More Creative Thinking

Now that you have a good start on your Opportunity Lists let's take some time developing additional networking strategies.

This is initial research only. Your networking opportunities should be reviewed on a weekly basis.

Do not join any group or send out any letters until you have completed the entire 10 day plan. You want to make sure that you are completely prepared with the appropriate tools prior to introducing yourself to potential employers or networking groups.

Join a Professional Group

By joining a group of professionals in your field of interest you are much more likely to hear about openings before they are made public.

The business section of your local newspaper usually has a listing of professional group meetings along with a contact number. (I've seen many listed in my local paper for sales professionals, marketing professionals, computer systems professionals, etc.) Your local Chamber of Commerce is also a good information source.

Don't overlook groups such as the Rotary or Kiwanis. There are also many professional men and women networking groups.

When you attend meetings your goal is to inform people that you are pursuing a new job opportunity, but remember, don't beat them over the head with requests. People become uncomfortable if you come across as desperate (and you are NOT desperate, you are going to be fine).

Attend Speeches

In my local paper there are regular listings of speeches being given by various professionals. For example, last year the National Association of Women Business Owners sponsored a speech by the local manager of Raytheon.

Even if you don't have an opportunity to talk directly to the person, by hearing them speak you will have a nice introduction for a cover letter ("I enjoyed your speech last week at the Professional Roundtable . . ."). Plus, you will certainly gain insight into the company.

Attend Job Fairs and Career Fairs

Job fairs and career fairs are usually well attended which means attended by you and a thousand others. Don't let the crowds discourage you. The chances of actually spending any quality time with a company representative may be slim, but these fairs can be a good place to pick up information about various companies and to drop off your resume face-to-face. You can gather lots of company representative business cards that will provide an opening to use in your cover letters, giving the reader a sense of familiarity ("I spoke briefly with Mark Smith at the Aerospace Career Fair in Denver . . .").

Contact Federal and State Agencies

There are opportunities through Federal and State agencies for re-training, job search assistance, etc. In Appendix I you will find information on how to contact these types of agencies.

Do not get discouraged when trying to discover what help may be available to you through the government. Everyone hits the same roadblocks when dealing with the government bureaucracy. Keep pursuing all that you are entitled to, but don't depend on this avenue for the greatest opportunities. Do yourself a favor, if you've spent a couple of hours trying to gather information and haven't been success-ful, drop it for the rest of the day and move on to another project.

Research Employment Agencies, Executive Search Firms

An effective job search requires investigating every available network-ing option, and employment agencies and recruiters are an option. It doesn't cost anything to learn what they have to offer. If there is a fee involved, make sure that it is fully paid by the employer.

Employment Agencies/Head Hunters

Usually agencies/head hunters specialize in a career field (engineering, sales, information technology, etc.). The agency/head hunter has two ways of payment: fee paid by the applicant or fee paid by the employer. Ask which payment method is used prior to agreeing to work with an agency.

Career Consulting Firms

These companies help you with the specifics of your job search includ-ing items such as resume writing and interview preparation. However most do not contact employers on your behalf. Be very careful that you receive a complete listing of the services these companies provide before you sign on.

Once again, if you organize your job search correctly, you should not be in the position of having to pay someone to find you a job.

Follow the Want Ads (newspapers and Internet)

You could spend all your time doing nothing but reading newspaper and Internet wants ads and forum discussions. Check them daily. Send in your resume to opportunities that appear interesting. However, these listings are a miniscule part of your job search. Do not depend on them for regular, solid leads.

Chapter Summary

❑ Organize and gather supplies for your workspace.

❑ Design your letterhead and business cards.

❑ Develop your Opportunity Lists.

❑ Begin to research networking opportunities in your area through the Internet, newspapers, magazines and trade journals.

Understanding the Interviewing Process and Self-Evaluation

CHAPTER GOALS

- Part I: To understand the reasoning behind the interview.
- Part II: To understand your role in the interviewing process through Self-Evaluation.
- Part III: To learn to discuss your problem areas in a professional manner.

A great deal of job search stress comes from fear of the unknown. Nowhere is stress more evident than on the day of an interview! What are they going to ask? Why are they asking these questions? What do they want from me?

Today you will learn what your role is in the interview and what responsibilities the interviewer may be facing.

The extensive Self-Evaluation Exercises will then help you discover answers to interview questions; deliver these answers in a concise, yet complete manner; and help you to discuss your problem areas in a professional manner.

These two topics are so important you will be spending the next two days focusing on them.

Part I: Understanding the Interview Process

For almost any type of position, the interviewer will want the following questions answered during the selection process. Does this applicant:

- Possess the technical skills needed for this position?
- Have the ability to clearly communicate ideas?

- ◆ Employ strong listening skills?
- ◆ Have an overall positive attitude about work and life in general?
- ◆ Appear to have an ability to adapt to new situations?
- ◆ Appear to have the ability to be a positive influence within the company?

The only person who can answer these questions is YOU. For this reason you must be prepared to fulfill your role of *information giver*. To stand out from the rest of the applicant crowd you must be prepared to share specific examples of your behavior. You need to come up with "stories" to tell in response to interview questions.

Example

Describe a conflict you had with a co-worker.

Applicant #1: No-Information Answer

I can't think of a specific conflict that I've had with a coworker. But, if I did encounter one, I feel the way to handle it is to talk to the person right away about our conflict.

Sounds good, but why should the interviewer believe that you would actually handle it that way?

Applicant #2: "Information Giver" Answer

I volunteered to work on a committee that reviewed cost cutting measures suggested by employees. The group I worked with was headed by one of our senior mechanics.

There was another employee on the committee who was an attorney from the company's legal department. She was not there to provide legal expertise; she was simply a member of the committee.

Every time we would review a suggestion she would find some tiny legal reason why the suggestion might not work. One afternoon we reviewed about ten very creative suggestions and she dismissed them all. I then made the comment to the group that perhaps we need not, especially at the beginning, be concerned about the legalities of a suggestion but to allow the best ideas to be sent up to the next level.

Well, it was pretty obvious that my comment was directed to her. She became very quiet and I realized I had embarrassed her. During lunch I took her aside and apologized to her. My comments, although well meaning, were completely misplaced and I should have voiced my concerns to her privately.

> Your role is to be a good *information giver.*

> *She was very gracious and accepted my apology. But, she also kept her legal positions to herself a little bit better.*

This story allows me to clearly visualize this person as a member of a team. I can also see the reason for his initial irritation and his inappropriate behavior. This story also shows me someone who is honest about his shortcomings and is not too ego-driven to apologize.

(Later today I will help you uncover your stories.)

The Interviewer

The approach an interviewer takes in an interview depends a great deal on his or her personality. Therefore, the interview can range from extremely formal to comfortably professional. It can be casual, hostile, or subtly intimidating.

No specific interviewer approach is more uncomfortable or difficult than another if you understand what approach *you* must take.

Your interview manner must never deviate from being formal, friendly, and positive. You must never take the interviewer's style personally. Wear this formal, friendly approach like a bubble that insulates you from external influences. You must consciously think about maintaining this formal, friendly and positive approach throughout the interview. Without this conscious effort it can be easy to fall into the trap of mirroring the interviewer's demeanor. (We sometimes respond in kind to the approach people take towards us in our daily lives. A rude salesclerk makes us feel on edge, and we most likely would not respond warmly to this person.)

Let's look at some common interviewing styles you might find during your job search.

Casual, Relaxed

The casual style of interviewing can be extremely effective for an interviewer.

The interviewer leans back in his chair, sips coffee, and uses a conversational tone of voice and method of questioning:

> *"I see you've worked with some fairly big corporate accounts for the past year, including MCD Corporation. I worked for them for three years and really enjoyed it. But, boy, they have lots of red tape don't they?"*

Suddenly, the applicant feels as though he is having coffee with a friend discussing mutual acquaintances. In this atmosphere the applicant may be more prone to offer information that is best left unoffered.

"You're right about that. They require fifty percent more paperwork than is necessary. It really becomes a chore after awhile, plus it is so wasteful."

Oops, now you could be viewed as talking negatively about your former employer, when it feels like all you are doing is chatting with a new friend.

Many years ago, I had a good friend who finally landed an interview with a company he had been pursuing for several months. He called me after his interview full of high spirits. "It went great!" my friend said, "I felt so comfortable with the interviewer we even talked about that problem I had at work last year."

Ouch! That problem had been resolved but the situation was one that did not put my otherwise tolerant friend in a very good light. I could only guess what else had been discussed. I groaned inwardly, knowing the outcome would not be positive. (It wasn't.)

Aggressive, Intimidating

The interviewer starts by surprising the applicant with a question such as:

"Although you have over ten years experience in the field, I am troubled by the fact that you have been unemployed for three months. Can you explain to me, Mr. Brown, why you haven't been offered a job?"

This type of questioning could put the unprepared applicant immediately on the defensive and may elicit a response that is equally aggressive:

*"Well, **sir,** you are incorrect in assuming I have not been offered a job. I was offered a very good position but it would have required a move and I choose not to do that."*

Every response you give to an interviewer is immediately viewed as the way you will handle yourself on a daily basis. If you are unable to maintain a professional demeanor during an interview (when you are supposed to be on your best behavior) what does that say about how you will react when you are on your own? Consequently, when you answer in an aggressive manner, the interviewer may feel as though you will not be able to conduct yourself professionally during periods of even minor stress.

When interviewers are aggressive it does not necessarily mean that they are concerned about a specific item in your background. Many times they simply want to see how an individual reacts when confronted with hostility.

Disinterested, Disorganized

The interviewer does not smile and the handshake seems insincere. He seems to only ask those questions that are written down in front of him.

The interviewer may be disorganized. He can't find your resume or your cover letter. Perhaps he will think of something he needs to do in the middle of the interviewer and leave the office for several moments. He may even take a phone call and chat for several minutes while you quietly sweat in your chair.

The best approach to this style is, as always, a friendly and professional manner. Don't try to lighten the mood with a joke or too much small talk.

If the interview is interrupted remember what you were discussing. Many times the interviewer will return and ask, "Where were we?" They usually know, but are checking to see if you were paying attention.

Mixed Bag

It is not uncommon for an interview to begin in one tone (casual) and suddenly change to a different tone (aggressive).

I spoke with one individual who interviewed with the company of his dreams. The interview process consisted of speaking one-on-one with several individuals within the company.

> *"It started out so casual and friendly. The first interviewer was extremely complimentary about my experience and education. He did not ask one question that I found difficult or uncomfortable.*
>
> *All that changed when I sat down with the second interviewer. He questioned not only my education but also said things like, 'It is interesting to me that you have not yet been given an account of a company that grosses over three million dollars annually.' This gave me the impression that he felt I was lagging behind my contemporaries. It was a little hard, but I just kept telling myself that this was all part of the process. I simply answered his questions as best I could. After about a half hour he lightened up. By the end of the interview I felt as though he approved of me. I was offered the job!"*

How different the outcome could have been if he'd lost his focus and taken the questioning personally.

Part II: Self-Evaluation Worksheet

Now that you have a basic understanding of the interviewing process, let's move on to the all-important Self Evaluation Exercises.

These extensive Self-Evaluation Exercises will help you: 1) Discover stories to use in response to questions you will be asked, 2) Deliver these stories in a concise, yet complete manner and, 3) Discuss your problem areas in a professional, straightforward manner.

My job is to ask you questions to help stimulate your memory concerning specific situations that you have faced. Your job is to take the time to really sift through your experiences and select stories that best describe your outlook and talents.

Discover Your Stories

These exercises will help you recall specific conflicts, work and personal decisions, and problems encountered during your lifetime. You will begin to understand how, and why, you have reacted in various situations. You will also learn how these lessons have helped you improve your performance in communication, leadership, team orientation, and decision-making.

Deliver Your Stories

These techniques will teach you how to deliver your stories. By following these guidelines, your stories will be more organized and full of appropriate information while at the same time taking less time to tell.

Discuss Your Problem Areas

These guidelines will help you discuss any potentially troublesome point or difficult issue in a professional, calm manner.

As you work through these exercises, remember:

Take Your Time

To be competitive you must discover and critique your stories well in advance of the interview. Trying to come up with applicable stories on the spot can be extremely difficult.

Each person will have a different opinion on the difficulty of these exercises. Some will find it fairly easy and, within two days, will have a basketful of stories to tell. Others may have to spend more time reviewing these exercises before they feel comfortable and ready for an interview.

Whatever category you find yourself in, given enough time, you will remember many appropriate stories.

Make No Comparisons

As you work through these exercises it is vitally important to remember we are all different! In the course of preparing for your interviews, it is important to learn about the competition. Only by researching a company's requirements and understanding what others might bring to a position will you know what areas to highlight on your resumes, cover letters and during an interview.

It is poor use of your days to spend precious time comparing yourself to others. It is human nature to be your own worst critic! Too much comparison will give you unrealistic opinions of your competition. Just as we all have special talents, we all also have problem areas. No matter how intellectually or physically attractive your competition appears I guarantee you they have weaknesses also.

Companies do not waste their time interviewing people who do not appear to be qualified. If you have been invited for an interview, rest easy knowing the company feels you may be the person to fill their needs. An interviewer will review the applicant's strengths and weaknesses and make the decision based on the applicant's total package.

> *I remember two clients I worked with several years ago. Bob had graduated at the top of his class, was tall, handsome, and dressed like a model. Initial impressions were wonderful. After spending some time with him, it became apparent that he was more impressed with himself than anyone else. He was eager to talk about his successes but unwilling to fully discuss his failures or mistakes.*
>
> *About a month later Joe, an acquaintance of Bob's, had an appointment with me. Joe was extremely nervous because Bob had yet to receive any job offers. Joe's approach was, "If Bob, with all his obvious advantages, is having trouble, what chance do I have?"*
>
> *It was true that Joe's academic achievements were not as stellar as Bob's, and he didn't dress as expensively. He was, however, much more personable, had a great attitude, and was able to discuss his entire background in detail. He offered an employer a terrific overall package and was offered a position at his first-choice company. (Bob was finally offered a position but it took him six months.)*

The following exercises will help you recognize all the strengths you possess and become comfortable discussing your weaknesses. Take your time. Be honest, but kind, to yourself.

Discover Your Stories

The first way to begin to discover your stories is to think about the people in your life. By reminiscing about past bosses, co-workers, teachers, friends, students, employees, etc., you will begin to remember shared experiences which will result in applicable stories to use in an interview.

> *Carl. Hmm, I haven't thought about him in years! Dealing with Carl was hard at the beginning. I remember that unexpected project we had to work on together and how we had completely different approaches. We worked late one night and the subject turned toward the tension that was between us. We realized the irritation was mutual and decided to make sure we were always absolutely clear with each other and thereby kept misunderstandings to a minimum. From then on, when we worked together, we always completed projects ahead of schedule.*

Great! Now you have a specific story to share when an interviewer asks you discuss a conflict with a co-worker. This story would give insight into your ability to communicate and adapt.

Let's review the areas that potential employers are going to be interested in.

Technical Knowledge
Interviewers Reasoning

There is one certainty in every interview: If you are not technically qualified you will never get to the point where you are asked to talk about yourself in other areas. For this reason, one of the first orders of business is to make sure your technical abilities are highly competitive.

The questions the interviewer must have answered are: How can this person help our company? Does this person know his "stuff"?

Does This Person:
   * Possess the fundamental knowledge necessary for this position, and/or do they have an above average knowledge of the job?
   * Need much training to assimilate into this position and into our company?
   * Have the ability to learn and apply new information quickly?

Ask Yourself:
   * What talents or training do I have for this job?
   * What innate abilities do I possess that make me successful in this line of work?

- What specific skills are needed for this job? Do I have all these skills? If yes, how did I acquire them? If no, what skills am I lacking and why?
- Which skills have I used in my past job? Have I been awarded special recognition or promoted for any of these skills?
- What skills do I possess that do not readily appear to be needed in this job but, nevertheless, have assisted me in excelling in this field?
- Besides the basic skills needed for the job, what additional skills have I acquired along the way? How have I incorporated these additional skills into my daily job activities?

Sample Interview Questions—Technical Ability

- Tell me about your background for this position.
- How did you learn this industry/skill?
- How would your past employers rate you? Why would they rate you that way?
- What are your greatest professional strengths/weaknesses?
- Why should we hire you over other people with the same basic qualifications?
- Rate what you feel are the most important aspects of this job.
- Describe what you believe would be a typical day in this position.

Attitude

Interviewer's Reasoning

Interviewers must feel confident the new employee will fit easily into the corporate environment. They want an employee who is easy to work with and someone who truly enjoys the type of work required for the position.

An employee with a positive attitude is invaluable to any employer. A positive attitude can make working overtime on a project, dealing with customer complaints, and handling daily internal emergencies less stressful for everyone. A positive attitude lays the groundwork for good communication and positive team interaction.

An employee who loves the work he performs will, obviously, be a happier person. This is why it is so important for an employer to ascertain if the applicant truly wants to work within the specific industry.

Asking questions about problem areas and life goals is a great way to gauge someone's true attitude.

Does This Person:
- Take responsibility for mistakes, or make excuses?
- Answer questions in a straightforward manner or use the question as a forum to discuss unfair treatment?

- Appear to have the ability to get along with others?
- Appear to have career goals?
- Show enthusiasm when discussing past job experiences?

Ask Yourself
- What difficulties have I faced during my lifetime (illness in the family, challenges funding education, etc.)? How did I get through these difficult times? What specific steps did I take to solve these problems?
- What has been my biggest disappointment? How did I handle this disappointment?
- What mistakes have I made on the job? How did I rectify them?
- What mistakes have I been unable to resolve? Why?
- How do I feel about past jobs and employers?
- What do I like about this field? What do I dislike?
- What is my basic outlook on life? Have I found it easy to get along with my fellow employees or have I had problems? What caused those problems?
- If there have been problems working with co-workers, what steps did I take to improve in this area?

Sample Interview Questions—Attitude
- Why are you interested in this field?
- How do you feel about your last employer?
- Can you tell me about a conflict that you have had with someone you supervised? With a co-worker/supervisor?
- Have you ever felt that a company policy was unfair to you? What did you do about it?

Communication
Interviewer's Reasoning

Good communication allows work to be completed on time, with fewer errors, and in a comfortable atmosphere where people understand their responsibilities. The ability to communicate can be especially important during times of stress and conflict.

Does This Person:
- Have the ability to keep the lines of communication open and flowing no matter what the situation or personalities involved?
- Have the ability to solve a conflict without causing new problems?
- Have the confidence to take constructive criticism?

- Have the confidence to speak up if he doesn't understand something?
- Express ideas clearly, concisely, and willingly?
- Appear to be a good listener?

Ask Yourself:
- What conflicts (large or small) have I had with co-workers? (Think of misunderstandings and differences of opinions.) What specific steps did I take to handle the conflict?
- What conflicts have I had with past employers? What steps did I take to handle the conflicts? How were the conflicts resolved?
- Were there any conflicts that I was never able to fully resolve? What were the reasons for my inability to resolve these conflicts? How would I handle the conflicts differently?
- Have I ever found myself stuck in the middle of a conflict between two other people? What did I do?
- What specific steps do I take when I find myself involved in a conflict?
- How would my peers/supervisors/family describe me?

Sample Interview Questions—Communication
- Tell me about a conflict you have had with an employee/co-worker/supervisor.
- Have you ever been counseled at work? Why?
- Tell me about a problem that you caused at work. Were you able to resolve the problem? Why or why not?
- What types of people do you like/dislike working with?

Team Orientation
Interviewer's Reasoning
Every position requires interaction with co-workers, clients, or customers.

Does This Person:
- Contribute to a positive, cooperative workplace?
- Appear sensitive to the feelings of others?
- Have the ability to handle conflicts without causing additional problems?

Ask Yourself:
- Outside of work when have I been a part of a team (community service, sports, committees)?
- When have I worked as a part of a team at work?

- What success/problems did I have while working as part of a team?
- Was I ever the individual who came up with a solution while working as part of a team? How did I suggest this solution? Was it the final solution? Why or why not?

Sample Interview Questions-Team Orientation

- Describe a team project.
- What do you dislike about working as part of a team? Why?
- What feedback did receive on your performance as a team member?
- How many people do you have to interact with on a daily basis? What types of problems do you encounter working with these individuals?

Adaptability

Interviewer's Reasoning

As we all know, things never seem to go as planned. Possessing the ability to adapt your behavior to diverse work styles and to differing environments is a must.

Does this person:

- Adjust to setbacks and have the ability to plan for change?
- Have the ability to think creatively when confronted with a setback or problem?
- Appear willing to lend a hand when extra work is needed due to an unforeseen situation?

Ask Yourself—Adaptability

- How have I reacted to the challenges of being laid off (if applicable)? What changes have I had to make? How have I made them?
- Have I ever offered my assistance when it was not expected of me?
- Have I ever had to work with someone whose work habits were distractions to me? How did I handle this situation?

Sample Interview Questions—Adaptability

- How do you feel about being laid off?
- Can you tell me about an unexpected problem that you encountered at work? What happened?
- Tell me about an unexpected deadline you experienced. How did you meet the deadline?

Deliver Your Story

Now that you have collected lots of stories, it is time to learn to effectively tell those stories.

There are two guidelines to follow when telling your stories:

- Divide each story into three parts: beginning middle, and end.
- You should attempt to complete each story in two minutes or less. (Stop reading and time two minutes. It's a long time!)

> *A client was trying to tell me about a work problem he had solved. He was only halfway through after speaking for five minutes. At the six-minute mark he stopped, blushed beet red, and said, "Oh, my gosh. I can't even remember what my point was!"*

The following guidelines will help your stories become more organized, include more pertinent information, and still take less time to tell.

The Beginning

Purpose: To set the scene.

The circumstances (time, place, your experience level) surrounding the story must be clear to the interviewer. Because you are familiar with the situation it is easy to leave out pertinent information.

For instance, a department manager with 15 years of experience is asked to give an example of a work problem and describe how he solved it:

The No-Information answer might begin:

> *"I came into work one morning and discovered a problem..."*

This person has 15 years of experience with three different companies. What company was he working for when this occurred? Did this happen when he was a sales representative, or a sales manager? We cannot tell from this type of response.

The Story Answer would state:

> *"I had just been promoted to manager at ABC Company. We were almost finished with a month-long project expanding our marketing plan to include four new states. On Friday afternoon a problem developed . . ."*

This second example shows the time and place (at the beginning of his tenure at his last company) and experience level (new manager).

> **Make your points in two minutes or less.**

Examples of No-Information beginnings vs. Story Answer beginnings:

"When I was in college" vs. *"It was the beginning of my junior year in college."*

"At my last company" vs. *"During my first month at ABC Company."*

"It was a busy time of year" vs. *"It was the holiday season when we do sixty percent of our annual business."*

"I was in the middle of a case" vs. *"I had been working for three months on the largest civil case I had ever been assigned."*

The Middle

Purpose: To provide only the major events of the story. To present these events in chronological order.

We have all listened to poor storytellers recount an experience. These people leave out information or fail to tell the story in an organized manner. They verbally jump around the story hopelessly trying to fill in the blanks in a failing attempt to explain their experience more clearly. The listener cannot follow the storyteller's train of thought and, after a while, tires of even trying. Being a poor storyteller can cause real disaster in an interview.

Interviewer:

"Tell me about a conflict you had with a co-worker."

The poor Story Answer:

"We had a new bookkeeper that had been with the company about a month. You know, I thought he was very aloof when I first met him, and he didn't really go out of his way to be friendly, so I thought maybe he was just shy. Anyway, in my department we had been having trouble with the cash register being short, so I put out a memo that no one was allowed into the cash register except the person working the register. I didn't think anyone was stealing or anything but I figured this way I could backtrack and find out where the mistakes were being made. Well, one day I came in late to work. I'd had a doctor's appointment-no, wait, it was a dentist. Anyway, I was working behind the desk and he came out and went over to the register and opened it and started taking out some cash. I showed him the memo I had sent. He said, "This is my job and I can go into any register any time I want to, no matter what you say!" Well, I was really embarrassed because there were customers milling around. It was one of the busiest times of the day and there were usually about 20 to 30

people in the area during that time that could hear us! I really thought this was an inappropriate response on his part and told him so, and he yelled even louder."

This person's delivery does not set the scene for us at all (What was his position? How long had he been with the company?). Also, there is a lot of information that is not needed to understand the story (I thought he was aloof, I had a doctors appointment, there are usually twenty people in the area). Plus, he left us not knowing how the situation was ultimately resolved (Did they talk later? Did he complain to his boss? Did he yell back?).

The Story Answer would be much clearer:

Beginning: *"When I was promoted to Manager of Customer Service at ABC Company . . ."*

Middle: *"I inherited a cash register problem. The cash register behind the Front Desk was always short by about $150.00 each evening. To try to figure out the problem, I sent a memo to all employees that no one was to use the cash register except the clerk on duty and myself.*

We had a new bookkeeper that had been with the company for about two weeks. I did not know him well. I came into work one afternoon and he was using the register. I approached him and said something like, 'Did you get my memo about the register?'

He immediately became very upset and said, 'This is my job and I can get into this register whenever I need to!'

I was extremely surprised by his response. He was quite loud, which was embarrassing to me since there customers nearby."

So far this story flows nicely. The storyteller is keeping the information organized and is providing the interviewer with solid information about his individual approach to handling conflicts.

The End

Purpose: To resolve any conflict of technical problem that occurred during the story.

If you do not provide an ending to your story, the interviewer will do it for you. The interviewer cannot assume anything positive, so it will not be a happy ending.

You must always take your story to the end. The end of the story comes when the problem is solved or when you had done all you possibly could to work through the problem.

If the cash register story stopped right now, the interviewer would be wondering: What was the final result? Did they resolve the conflict or did the problem simmer and the tension increase?

The organized Story Answer would end the story.

> **End:** *"I said, 'Let's go back to my office.' As we walked through the reception area to my office, he continued to talk very loudly about how I had no right to tell him what to do.*
>
> *When we were alone I said, 'There are two things we need to talk about. One is the cash register situation, and the other is how you reacted to me just now.' I told him certainly I would want to know when he was upset with me, but I would prefer he speak to me in private. I told him I meant nothing personal by asking him to not use the register; I had requested this of everyone. Well, he calmed down fairly quickly and apologized at the end of our talk, which took about five minutes. We then talked about the register problem and agreed on some tactics to solve the problem. I realized he was extremely volatile so I never spoke to him about problems unless we were in private. That seemed to work well."*

Excellent. I see this person as organized and having a professional approach towards handling difficult situations.

Use visualization when telling a story. Place yourself back in the situation; see yourself working through the problem. By visualizing the situation you will find it easier to offer the information in an organized manner.

People tend to be long-winded because they repeat themselves or add information that is not applicable to the discussion. To help alleviate this problem, listen to what you are saying. If you hear yourself repeating a point or perhaps talking about something that has nothing to do with the question asked-move on! It will certainly make everyone happy if you just stop, say something like, "Excuse, me, I am off-track, my point is . . ." and get back to the point of your story.

Part III: Problem Areas

If you are like me, as you worked through the Self-Evaluation Worksheet you were forced to notice problems you have had during your career. These could be problems that were thrust upon you, or it could be that you were the source of the problem.

For almost everyone, discussing one's faults and mistakes is an anxiety-producing part of an interview. However, areas of weakness or failures do not have to be overwhelmingly difficult to discuss.

Everyone has personal situations they would rather not discuss. It makes no difference if the applicant is twenty years old with one year of work experience or fifty years old with thirty years of experience—both have skeletons in their closets. The severity of the problems may vary but the level of discomfort is always high.

Don't fool yourself into thinking that the interviewer might overlook a problem area. An important part of the interviewer's job is to search out and dissect an applicant's past failures and areas of weakness. Your problem areas *will* be topics of discussion.

One of the worst mistakes you can make during an interview is to show irritation, frustration, or defensiveness toward the interviewer. These reactions most commonly surface when an individual is caught unprepared or unwilling to discuss a problem area. To neutralize this minefield, you must face those areas you would prefer never to discuss (or think about!) again. A thorough, honest examination of past mistakes will allow you to:

◆ Desensitize yourself, as much as possible, to the situation.
◆ Know the exact words you want to use when explaining the situation.
◆ Anticipate follow-up questions.
◆ Point out what you have learned and how you have improved.
◆ Ultimately discover that, often, the anticipation is far worse than the actual questioning.

Take Responsibility

A mature individual takes responsibility for past mistakes. An applicant who tries to rationalize a mistake is viewed as immature and irresponsible.

> You must take responsibility for past mistakes.

Several years ago I met with two new clients in the same afternoon. One client had been fired from a previous job, and the other client had been in the job search for over six months. Although being unemployed for such a long period of time was going to be a serious topic of discussion, I felt that the termination issue would be a far more difficult hurdle to overcome.

After spending time with these two clients, I reversed my opinion.

The individual who had been terminated came prepared and ready to discuss the situation. He presented me with letters of recommendation from past employers, an explanation from the terminating employer's perspective, and his own written explanation. He was calm, straightforward and professional during our twenty-minute discussion. Although the fact still remained that he had been terminated, I felt confident an interviewer would give him every consideration.

At all his interviews time was spent discussing his termination. His past employer was always called for a reference. But, because of his professional approach he found himself in the position of having several choice job offers from which to choose.

In sharp contrast the second applicant refused to admit that he had any responsibility for being unemployed for six months. He pointed the finger at everyone but himself. When I asked him why he thought he wasn't getting job offers he talked about favoritism, nepotism, and a host of other reasons he believed relieved him of any responsibility for his situation. Although technically and educationally well qualified, he could never seem to make it past an initial interview. (Although he was offered many excellent interview opportunities based on his experience, he eventually had to take a position of lesser responsibility at about half his former salary. Not surprising!)

When discussing a problem area, tell the complete story and accept responsibility for your actions.

Know Exactly How You Want to Explain the Situation.

Sit down and confront the problem. Relive the situation and critique what went wrong. Where did the problem start? What events led to the final outcome?

Try to look at the problem from all points of view. For example, if you were terminated, critique not only your own feelings, but also try to look at the situation from your employer's perspective. Decide what details are needed to clearly explain the situation. Write out what you want to say. Your complete handwritten explanation should take up no more room than the front and back of a 3 x 5 index card.

With enough editing even the most complicated problem can be explained in two minutes or less.

At the end of your two minute explanation, offer to answer any questions. End with a comment such as, "I hope I have explained the situation clearly. I am happy to answer any questions you may have."

Question
"Could you explain why you were terminated from your last position?"

Negative Response
"The reason I was given was that I was late too many times. I was never more than 15 or 20 minutes late, and everyone else did it. Anyway, that was the reason I was given."

At least the applicant gave the real reason. Too bad she didn't take responsibility for it.

Positive Response

"As the Office Manager it was my responsibility to open up the office for the day. I was new to this type of professional position and the company atmosphere was very casual. People pretty much came and went at will. I was really the only one in the office that needed to be there at a regular time. But I still thought since everyone else didn't follow the clock, so could I. My boss did warn me once and my behavior changed a bit. But, I then moved to a new apartment that was farther away from work and allowed myself to think this offered me an excuse to be late.

Because I was responsible for opening up the office in the morning it set a bad tone for others to have to do that part of my job.

I had the ability to control my arrival time but didn't. I can tell you that I learned a very important lesson from this experience. It is no fun being terminated for something you could control. I sat down and had a long talk with myself and came up with some ideas for time management. This is never going to happen again."

This is an honest, straightforward response to a legitimate question. Because of the professional response I would suspect that this applicant will be critiqued on her overall skills package and not dismissed because of one error in judgment.

Remember, you do not have to offer information about weaknesses or problem areas until you are asked. But, it is important to be prepared to discuss all your problem areas.

Practice Your Delivery

There is a funny scene in an old Cary Grant movie *My Favorite Wife*. Cary is calling his second wife, whom he just married that day, to explain that his first wife has just returned home after having been marooned on an island for seven years. As he waits for Wife #2 to answer the phone, he nervously delivers his explanation of the situation under his breath. It sounds perfect.

However, as soon as he hears her voice over the phone, he becomes completely unnerved, forgets what he wanted to say, and becomes so flustered he hangs up on her, which, of course, only makes things worse.

No matter how good your explanation sounds in your head, I guarantee it will not sound so terrific the first couple of times you verbalize it. So, practice your delivery.

Be Aware of Your Body Language.

When discussing problem areas, body language becomes particularly important. It is imperative that you maintain good eye contact that your voice remains strong, and your hands and legs remain relaxed.

By knowing what you want to say you will automatically be calmer and more relaxed.

Chapter Summary

❏ Your role in the interview is to be a good information giver.

❏ Never take the interviewer's approach personally.

❏ It takes Self-Evaluation to discover and deliver your stories in a professional manner.

❏ In order to increase your chances of overcoming a problem in your past, you must take responsibility for the problems you have encountered in your career.

Company Research and Job Skills Enhancement

CHAPTER GOALS

- ◆ To become proficient in researching companies of interest.
- ◆ To make sure your job skills are at their best.

Company Research

A friend called one evening to fill me in on the job interview he had attended that day. "It was going great until they asked me if I had ever been to the city where the company's headquarters were located. I didn't have a clue as to where their headquarters were. I could tell they were not impressed, and that I had just blown a pretty good opportunity."

It will be impossible to talk intelligently about what you can do for a company until you know what they need.

If you understand the company's needs it will be much clearer what areas of your background you should highlight on your resume and in an interview. For example, if you discover during your research that the company is planning to open offices in three new states, then it would make sense to mention that you have experience in setting up a new office, as you helped do that when your company opened a second branch.

Take out your Opportunity Lists. You should strive to answer the following questions for each company.

- ◆ What, *exactly*, does the company do? (I know this initially sounds stupid, but can you explain in ten words or less what the company does? If not, you should.)
- ◆ What is the history of the company?
- ◆ How long has the company been in business?
- ◆ Who started the company?

- How many employees are there?
- Where is the corporate office? Where are the satellite offices?
- Do they have a corporate philosophy (or corporate statement)?
- Who are the company officers (president, vice-presidents, etc)?
- What is the stock history (if applicable)?
- What is their biggest product/most valuable service?
- Who buys/uses their products, services, etc?
- Who are their biggest clients?
- Where does the company rank in comparison to the competition?
- Has the company ever had a dramatic increase or decrease in business? Why?
- What are the short- and long-term goals of the company?

Sources of Information

- Newspapers are an excellent source of current company information. To access city newspapers online start with a search engine such as Google or Yahoo and type in the name of the paper: Boston Herald, Denver Post, etc. Then enter the name of the company in the 'search' box.
- Regularly check the front page and business sections for news stories on your companies of interest. If you see a news item that reports a company just received a new contract for manufacturing 10 million jackets for the 2004 World Cup, now would be a good time to send in your resume to that company for a position of athletic clothes designer!
- Check out past articles in magazines and trade journals. If a magazine or trade journal is large enough you should be able to find past articles on their website.

  If you are unsure of which magazines to review simply start with a search engine such as Google or Yahoo and type in 'business magazines'. General business magazines in the genre of Barron's, Business Week, Fortune, etc. are a good place to start.

  Obviously trade journals will be specific to your area of interest. Once again use Google or Yahoo-type search engines and type in your specific trade: book publishing journals, engineering trade journals, teaching trade journals, etc.

- Don't overlook financial websites. Many offer 6-month, 2-year and 5-year stock history of the company. Reuters.com is a good site to kick off your research.

◆ Visit the company's website. To find the site use a search engine such as Google or Yahoo and then type in the specific company name.

On the company website many times you can find specific names of decision makers. This will be helpful if you are looking for people to contact to request informational interviews.

◆ Call or write for a company annual report. Many times you can find it online.

◆ Talk to past or current employees of the company. It would be ideal to talk with someone in the department where you would like to work, however, any employee can give you an overall view of the company.

◆ If possible, talk to customers of the company.

◆ If a company has a retail establishment visit one of their locations.

Most likely a great deal of your research will be done on the Internet. Let me share some search tips to help make good use of your time.

Internet Search Tips

◆ Define your objective for the day.

Don't just get on the Internet and start looking around; it is much too easy to become distracted! (Personally I have logged on to research the name of a book and two hours later have read all the latest movie reviews and have checked out the Guinness Book of World Records site.)

Decide what specific information you want to research that day. Are you looking for company research? Do you want to investigate a particular career field? Are you looking for specific career chat rooms where you can ask advice? Write down your priority for the day on a piece of paper and tape it to your computer. Don't get sidetracked!

◆ Avoid sites that ask for money.

There are plenty of job search strategies that cost nothing. Don't get caught up in thinking that just because you give someone money that they will do the work for you.

◆ Make sure that whenever you list personal information you are doing so on a secure site.

Job Skills Enhancement

As you have researched your companies of interest you have probably started to get a good idea of what potential employers are searching for. Now is the time to ask yourself the question: Are my skills in tip-top shape?

If you need to brush up on your technical skills; do it. If you need to reacquaint yourself with professional regulations; get the books out. If you will need to demonstrate your sales skills; do some role-playing selling the company product. If you will need to speak in front of a group; ask your friends over and give a talk.

Now is the time to brush up on your skills. You must be prepared to prove you possess excellent technical qualifications.

Using the following worksheet dissect the requirements of each specific position you are pursuing. Your goal is to develop a list of specific duties and responsibilities for each position.

By critiquing what skills and responsibilities you could face on a daily basis at your new job, and reviewing your past job responsibilities, you will be pleasantly surprised at how clear a picture you can form of what will be discussed during your interview.

Ask yourself

For each job you are pursuing answer the following questions (as best you can) prior to attending an interview.

What will my daily activities be?

What skills will I be called upon to use on a daily basis?

What is the bottom line of this job?

Let me give you an example of how a sales management applicant may approach these questions.

Sales Management Position

What will my daily activities be?
- Daily tracking of sales quotas.
- Assisting sales representatives with account problems.
- Handling account complaints the sales representatives are unable to handle.
- Summarizing sales progress to regional supervisor.

What skills will I be called upon to use on a daily basis?
- Motivation.
- Communication.
- Problem solving.

- ◆ Using computer software.
- ◆ Writing sales reports.

What would be the bottom line of my position?

- ◆ Increasing sales while maintaining morale.

Then, make sure your skills in these areas are in top form!

Chapter Summary

❏ You should be comfortable in conducting research on your companies of interest.

❏ You have compiled a solid list of information sources: magazines, newspapers, trade journals.

❏ You have dissected your potential job responsibilities.

❏ You are taking steps to ensure that your job skills are tip-top.

> Make sure your specific skills are at their best.

Paperwork Portrait

CHAPTER GOALS

- Collect Information required for applications and resume.
- Write your resume.

By now you have some good information on what type of position you want to pursue, what companies you may want to work for, along with what you have to offer your potential employer. Now it's time to put together resumes and cover letters that clearly and concisely highlight these facts.

I know this is the day you probably haven't been looking forward to. I'll do my best to make this as painless as possible.

Think in Specifics—Write Using Bullet Points.

When writing your resume and cover letters don't lose sight of the fact that these documents must provide the potential employer with proof that you have the talent to succeed in this position. In order to provide specific proof you must offer specific examples of your professional success. For example, if you were pursuing a sales position you would want to mention the following facts:

- #1 in sales at your former company.
- Salesperson of the Year two years running.
- Increased sales 25% during tenure with the company.
- Sales in my area were the highest in the company's history.

These facts would be highlighted through the use of bullet points. Each bullet point should highlight a proven fact that shows you are qualified for the position.

Sales Manager, ABC Company

Wrong:

Proven abilities within computer sales.

Right:

- Increased territory sales by 45% over the course of two years.
- Met or exceeded all sales quotas.

Design Manager, ABC Company

Wrong:

Responsible for hiring and managing all design staff.

Right:

- Recruited and managed design staff of 25 engineers, 12 safety technicians, 6 administrative staff, and 2 copywriters.
- Staff increased by 15 people during my tenure.
- Design Department experienced no turnover during my three years as manager.

Audit Staff Accountant, ABC Company

Wrong:

Researched technical accounting issues.

Right:

- Researched technical accounting issues. Implemented two new techniques for account processing which lowered department expenses by $75,000 per year.

Freelance Business Consultant, XYZ Company

Wrong:

Work with financially troubled companies.

Right:

- Work with financially troubled companies facing bankruptcy. Through reorganizing debt and working one-on-one with creditors 85% of clients are able to eliminate the need for bankruptcy filing.

Keep this bullet point process in mind as you work through the WORK HISTORY section.

Not every job lends itself to listing 'bullet point' successes so don't try. It is almost impossible to quantify successes in a job such as lifeguard, waiting tables, etc. However, my point in discussing this bullet-point approach is to make sure that if you DO have specific successes you don't forget to mention them (If you did save three people's lives as a lifeguard, mention it).

Information Collection Worksheet

Writing your resume and cover letters, filling out applications and gathering specific company requested paperwork is a task that requires complete accuracy. You will find the entire process much easier if you gather all required information prior to beginning the actual process of writing these documents.

Following is a list of information you most likely will need when writing your resume and covers letters or filling out a company application. Gathering this information before you begin writing will save you time and frustration in the long run. It is better to have too much information than constantly having to retrace your steps looking for background facts required by an application or employer.

Work History

◆ If you have been in the job market for five years or more list all your work history back to college or initial 'out of school' jobs. Include dates of employment, company name, job title and duties, and salary.

◆ If you are just starting out, list all jobs back to high school.

◆ Collect accurate addresses and phone numbers for all past employers. You will be surprised at how much information you can collect with a few phone calls. Do not go into an interview without being able to provide the potential employer with the necessary information for contacting your past employers. If you truly cannot find an address or phone number for a past employer, you must still be able to present some kind of documentation that you were employed. W–2s, employer critiques or a notarized letter from a fellow co-worker stating that you worked there will normally be sufficient.

◆ You never know what types of legal constraints are placed upon a business. For this reason gather as much information as possible about all past employment. This is especially true if you are pursuing a job that requires special security credentials.

◆ If a company application asks specifically why you left a past employer keep your explanation simple:
  • Company bankruptcy.
  • Layoff / industry slowdown.

- Termination. Complete explanation available upon request.
- To pursue other career options. Eligible for rehire. (Use this if you truly left the job because you wanted to. Eligible for rehire will allay any fears about a mutual decision to resign. Which an employer translates as 'terminated'.)
- If you and your employer mutually agreed you should resign you must be ready for the question, "Are you eligible for rehire?" Contact your former employer and make sure you know exactly what will be said about your situation should the potential employer call for a reference.

◆ If you have more than two months between jobs (when you were not in school), list what you were doing:
  - 6/98 to 4/99: Actively seeking employment.
◆ List any awards or achievements received through your employment. These facts can then be placed on your resume in the form of a bullet point.
  - Employee of the Month: July and August 2002.

Education

◆ List all your formal education. Include all degrees received and the area of study as well as the name of the school with city and state. If you have a college degree you need not list your high school education.
◆ List all education awards or achievements:
  - Graduated with 3.8 GPA (4.0 scale)
  - Recipient of Four-Year Hart Academic Scholarship for College Athletes
◆ If you paid for part or all of your education, list how this was accomplished.
  - Paid for all college and living expenses by working part-time and with financial assistance from winning the Hart Academic Scholarship.

Specialized Training

◆ List any specialized training. If your specialized training isn't within your field don't feel as though it isn't applicable information. Having an interest outside your field can help to paint you as a well-rounded person.

An applicant pursuing an insurance adjusters position lists:
  - Thirty college credits in Meteorology at Ohio State University.

An applicant pursuing a sales position lists:
- Ongoing Acting Studio and Fiction Writing Classes at WCC College.

These little snippets of information can provide more of a three-dimensional view instead of simply seeing that person as only a job applicant. Perhaps the potential employer will subconsciously view the applicant as a person who might have interesting things to talk about.

Community Involvement

- This could be an important part of your resume. List all past or present volunteer experience. Include your job titles, name of the organization and your basic duties.
  - Volunteer for the American Red Cross. On-call for local disaster relief such as fire, floods, etc.
- Don't overlook activities through your children's school.
  - Soccer Coach for past two years for the Middle School Monsters Soccer Team.
- List any awards received through your volunteer work.
  - The Patience Award given by the Middle School Monsters Soccer Team.

Interests or Hobbies

- Be specific if you have unusually in-depth interest or hobbies.
  - President of the Amateur Web Designers of America.
  - Past President of the ABC Airline United Way.

Additional Information

- Collect letters of reference from all past employers.
- Gather letters of recommendation from personal references.
- Make sure you have correct addresses and phone numbers for all references.

Resume Hints

- As a general rule you want to keep your resume to one page. You should never exceed two pages unless you have a list of published articles, research papers, or applicable specialized training.
- Use 25lb. 100% cotton paper. It is a safe bet to use an ivory colored paper. (White is ok, but it can be harsh on the eyes.)
- Use the same style and color of paper for your resume, reference sheet, and cover letter.
- Be consistent with abbreviations. If you abbreviate states (i.e., California to CA) then make sure you abbreviate each state name throughout the resume.
- Use letterhead stationary with your name, address, and phone number listed the same way it is on your resume.
- Do not use generic statements for your Objective. Each job you apply for should have a personalized resume.

  Wrong: Seeking a challenging position in customer service or management.

  Right: Manager of Customer Service for ABC Corporation.

  If you are pursuing a position that requires the same basic responsibilities (no matter what company) it is possible the only thing you need to change on your resume is the name of the company.

  However, if you are pursuing the same position within two different industries you may need to highlight different experience. If Company A uses Sales Elite Software and Company B uses Sales Giant Software you would want to highlight your expertise in Sales Elite for Company A and Sales Giant for Company B.

- Do not put the word "resume" on your resume.
- Do not list references on your resume. List them on a separate sheet of paper.
- Keep font styles simple. Do not use more than two different style fonts on your resume.
- Always include on your resume:
  - Objective
  - Work History (other titles such as Experience, Professional Background)
  - Education
  - (If applicable) Professional Affiliations or Specialized Training

- Leave off your birth date or age. Companies are very concerned about age-discrimination cases.
- Do not leave unexplained employment gaps of more than two months.
- Before sending out your resume and cover letter take the time to recheck:
    - Employment Dates.
    - Names, address, phone numbers.
    - Spelling, grammar and punctuation.

Resume Example

TERRY CULBERTSON
782 Great Job Road
Willcall, Colorado 85321
(450) 555-1212 (home), (450) 555-2121 (cell)
tculbertson@home.com

Objective

Convention Manager for Ruby Hotels

Experience

<u>Assistant Catering Manager</u>—Caron Hotels, Denver, Colorado
September 2000 to present.
Organized menu, wait staff schedules, beverage menu and cost structure for all hotel events. Presented plan to Catering Manager for final approval.
- Managed hotel's largest event during Catering Manager's absence: 5-day Convention for The Trial Attorneys of America (A of A). Over 5,000 guests attended the final dinner seating. Rec'd Letter of Appreciation from the Chairman of A of A.

<u>Administrative Assistant: Catering Department</u>—Caron Hotels, Denver, Colorado.
September 1998 to 2000.
Administrative Assistant for Assistant Catering Manager, Catering Manager, plus two Catering Sales Representatives. Responsible for final billing of all events.
- Promoted to Assistant Catering Manager on the recommendation of Catering Manager.

<u>Hotel Night Auditor</u>—Holiday Hotels, Denver, Colorado.
Part-time September 1996 to September 1998.
Responsible for night reconciliation of room and meal charges. Acted as Night Front Desk Clerk. Worked 11pm to 5am three days a week.
- Never missed a day of work in two years.

Education

B.A. in Business Administration, Minor: Hotel Management. University of Denver.
- Graduated with 3.6 (4.0 scale).
- Dean's List 1996 and 1997.
- Paid for college and living expenses by working within hotel industry.

References available upon request.

Opportunity List Letters

CHAPTER GOALS

- ◆ To complete letters for all individuals on your Opportunity Lists.

O K! You have your resumes pretty much written. Hopefully, you have also spent some time researching companies of interest. We are now ready to start using those Opportunity Lists.

The first step in putting your Opportunity Lists into play is to compose compelling, personalized letters to each person.

It's not as hard as it seems, I promise. The reality is you need only write one basic letter for each group. Then, it can be as simple as changing the name of the person to whom you are writing.

If you have trouble writing letters feel free to use my sample letters as your frame. The most important step is to get started. Write something! Once you have a basic letter written you can edit and personalize as required.

It may comfort you to know that this is not a creative writing test. No one is looking to be entertained. The most immediate need is to have the information presented in a direct, time efficient manner. For this reason you never want any letter to be more than one page.

> **None of your letters should be more than one page.**

Things to Keep in Mind

If relocation is a viable option you will also want to add an additional request into your Opportunity List letters. At this point you are open for an introduction to anyone who lives in that city. At the very least you can chat with them about the culture of the city, what fields seem to be expanding, etc. Once you become comfortable with these new 'long distance' contacts you can then add them to your Opportunity Lists and write them a letter asking for specific suggestions concerning your job search.

Ask your relocation contacts which local newspapers offer the best want ads and business section. Check these newspapers on a daily basis, paying particular attention to the weekend edition (usually more job listings on the weekends).

Try Very Hard to Not Put People on the Spot

During the course of your job search you need to inform people that you are conducting a job search; however don't beat them over the head with "I need a job!" People have a tendency to shut down when faced with a desperate person. So, keep your conversations light! Tell them, clearly and concisely, what type of job you are pursuing.

Negative

> *"I am looking for a job within website design. Even though there are a lot more businesses that offer this service, I can't seem to get my foot in the door. Do you know anyone you could introduce me to?"*

Positive

> *"I'm pursuing a position within website design. One of the things of interest to me is the number of businesses that offer web design. There are probably thirty percent more than even four years ago. Do you know anyone in this field?"*

Sample Letters for Opportunity Lists and Miscellaneous Job Search Letters

These basic letters can be used repeatedly for different positions. Please! Don't stress yourself out trying to be creative. Plagiarize from my letters as much as you want.

Opportunity List A

Letter for Friends and Relatives

With the people on this list you are going to:

- Send a letter or email describing your current job situation and listing exactly what types of positions you are pursuing.
- After you have given them a week to ruminate on your request you will call to ask if they have any suggestions.
- Keep them comprised of your progress through e-mails or short notes every six weeks or so.

Sample: Friend/Relative Letter

Steven Evans
456 West Phoenix Ave.
San Diego, California 85858
(845) 565-3830
stevenevans@aol.com

February 12, 2003

Captain Bill Jones
Friendly, Arizona

Dear Paul:

You are probably surprised to be receiving a formal letter from me. As you may not know, I was laid off last week due to my company's weak financial position. For this reason I am currently searching for a full-time position. (Although I also open to any part-time or temporary positions with the idea that they could possibly lead to full-time employment.)

I am actively pursuing specific opportunities within the security industry. To begin I should let you know exactly what my skills are and what opportunities seem to be a good match for me. As you review my background perhaps you may think of additional avenues I should pursue.

Some highlights of my background:
- B.A. in Law Enforcement
- Worked my way through college as a security guard for special events at ABC Stadium.
- In my work as an airline pilot I also volunteered my time to work on the Hotel Committee. Part of our responsibilities including visiting hotels to assure they met safety and comfort standards for our crews.

I see potential opportunities within companies that provide both home security and business security. Sales of security systems would also be a possibility. Another arena I am pursuing would be working within a specific company providing security. Department stores, hotels, and private businesses may need individuals with my background.

Paul, any suggestions you may have on how to optimize my job search would be greatly appreciated. I promise I will treat any referrals you give with the utmost professional courtesy. I have enclosed my resume for your review.

We've been through difficult times before and always come out ahead. This time will be no different. Thanks Paul, in advance, for any brilliant ideas you may have.

Sincerely,

Steven Evans

Opportunity List B

Business Acquaintances

With the people on this list you will:

- Send a letter (a letter is more formal) to each person describing in detail your job goals.
- Ask if they know anyone in your field to whom they would be comfortable referring you.
- Ask them to keep their eyes and ears open for any position within your field of interest, or a position closely related to your field. (You are looking for a full-time engineering position, and someone tells you of a two-week engineering consulting job.)
- After they have had the letter for a week, follow up with a personal phone call to discover if they have any ideas or suggestions.
- Keep them apprised of your progress through brief notes or emails every six weeks or so.

Sample: Business Acquaintances Letter

Samantha Evans
1345 E. Templeton Drive
Denver, Colorado 83838
(303) 555-3939, samantha@att.net

November 12, 2003

Mr. John Boss
Manager of Administration—Caron Hotels
Denver, Colorado

Dear Mr. Boss:

It was a pleasure meeting you at the Chamber of Commerce luncheon. I am writing to ask if you might have some insight or ideas as to current opportunities available within the Caron Hotels.

My college degree is in Business Administration. I paid my way through college by working for four years as a Night Auditor for the Merrit Hotel in Denver. I also acted as an on-call Front Desk Clerk. In this capacity I filled in when regular Front Desk employees were absent from work or when the hotel was filled to capacity. For the last four years I have been working within the travel industry as a Customer Service Representative for ABC Airlines.

I would like to ask for a few moments of your time to discuss my options. Any insight you could offer would be greatly appreciated. I will contact your office on Tuesday, October 5 to see if an appointment might be possible. Thank you very much for considering my request.

Respectfully,

Samantha Evans

Opportunity List C

Requesting Informational Interviews

With the people on this list you will:

- ◆ Write each person a formal business letter describing your goals.
- ◆ In the letter ask for 15 minutes (no more) of their time to discuss your plans and to ask for input on your job search and work goals. This is called an informational interview.
- ◆ Give a specific day when you will call to make an appointment. Do not fail to call on that day. They may be waiting for your call to give you some helpful advice.
- ◆ Before any informational interview make a list of specific questions you would like to ask. Do not go into your meeting without a specific agenda.
- ◆ Don't ask for a job. The person knows you are job hunting. If you approach him with, "Wanting to discuss my options," and not, "I need a job," he or she will feel more inclined to brainstorm with you instead of just reacting with, "Sorry, we have nothing at this time."
- ◆ Following your meeting, write a brief thank-you note. Mention any action you are going to take based on the suggestions the person gave you. The note should be no more than six or seven sentences.
- ◆ Keep the person notified of your progress through brief notes every six weeks or so.

Sample: Requesting Informational Interviews

Samantha Evans
148 East Avenue
Tucson, Arizona 85667
(520) 555-1212 (home), (520) 555-2222 (cell)
sevans2@ds.net

October 1, 2003

Mr. John Boss
Manager of Administration
Caron Hotels
Tucson, Arizona

Dear Mr. Boss:

My name is Samantha Evans and I am currently investigating specific opportunities with the hospitality industry. I am writing to ask for a few moments of your time to discuss your opinion of my options. I completely understand that Caron Hotels is not hiring at this time.

My college degree is in Business Administration. I paid my way through college by working for four years as a Night Auditor for the Marriott Hotel in Denver. I also acted as an on-call Front Desk Clerk. In this capacity I filled in when regular Front Desk employees were absent from work or when the hotel was filled to capacity and needed extra Front Desk assistance. For the last four years I have been working within the travel industry as a Customer Service Representative for BlueSky Airlines.

Thank you for considering my request for a meeting. I will contact your office on Tuesday, October 5 to see if a 15-minute appointment might be possible.

Respectfully,

Samantha Evans

If you have a personal introduction, make sure you use the person's name in the very beginning of the letter:

Dear Mr. Boss:

Richard Jones suggested that I contact you concerning my research into positions within the hospitality industry . . .

Informational Interviewing Sample Questions

An informational interview is just that: an interview to collect information.

Asking for an informational interview allows you to introduce yourself to business decision makers who are not actively hiring, or when you are looking to learn more about a company or industry.

Do not request an informational interview and then sit in front of the person and request a job! They will feel as though they have been duped. If you present yourself as a motivated and mature professional they may well keep you in mind should something in their company open up.

Start with general information questions and end with specific questions about your job interests.

- How did you get started with this company?
- What is your outlook for this field?
- What kind of attributes do you look for in an employee?
- Do you have any suggestions as to how I could improve my qualifications?
- Do you have any suggestions or ideas as to how to expand my job search opportunities?
- Do you have any ideas as to who may be hiring in the future?
- If you were in my shoes, what would be your next step?

Opportunity List D
Companies Currently Hiring
- You may send the same basic letter to different companies when you are applying for the same type of position.
- The areas you will want to individualize are (obviously) the position you are applying for and the highlights of your experience that relates to the specific company requirements.
- Once a company has had your resume or application for at least a week, you may call to follow up.

Sample: Companies Currently Hiring Letter

Thomas Culbertson
782 Great Job Road
Chicago, Illinois 85321
(450) 555-1212 (home), (450) 555-2121 (cell)
tculbertson@home.com

October 12, 2003

Mr. Bob Hire
Manager of Catering Services
Leisure Resort Hotel Companies
Chicago, Illinois

Dear Mr. Hire:

If the company is hiring:
I would like to submit my name for consideration for the position of Convention Sales

If you have a personal introduction:
Richard Thomas suggested I contact you about your need for a Convention Sales

If you read a want ad,
I read with interest the advertisement for Convention Sales in the 10/12/03 edition of the *Chicago Times*. As you can see from my resume I have extensive experience within Restaurant Supplies Sales.

My major was in Business Administration. During college I worked as the Assistant Catering Manager for Caron Hotels in Denver. As I am sure you are aware, Caron Hotels is one of the largest hotels in the Denver metropolitan area. My responsibilities in this position were varied and I learned a great deal, not only about catering and event planner, but also about the hotel and restaurant industry in general. In 1996 I began with XYZ Restaurant Supplies as a Sales Representative.

With the many contacts I have made in the business community within the last five years, I feel strongly I could immediately make a positive contribution to the Leisure Resort Hotel.

I hope after reviewing my qualifications you will deem it worthwhile to speak with me in person.

Sincerely,

Thomas Culbertson

Miscellaneous Letters

Sample: Thank You for Informational Interview

Samantha Evans
148 East Avenue
Tucson, Arizona 85667
(520) 555-1212 (home), (520) 555-2222 (cell)
sevans2@ds.net

October 12, 2003

Mr. John Boss
Manager of Caron Hotels
Tucson, Arizona

Dear Mr. Boss:

Thank you for meeting with me last Thursday.

As you suggested, I made changes to my resume and also contacted Mr. Willow with Embassy Hotel. He has graciously offered to speak with me this Thursday.

I am extremely encouraged about the opportunities I am uncovering. Thank you again for taking the time to speak with me. I will keep you informed as to my progress.

Respectfully,

Samantha Evans

Sample: Letter of Reference

Asking for a letter of recommendation can make you feel like you are imposing. To limit your intrusion on the person's time you could suggest that you write the basic letter. Then send it to them for editing, personalization and their signature.

To Whom It May Concern:

It is with pleasure that I write this letter of recommendation for Phil Jones.

Phil has been our Convention Sales Manager for the past two years. Throughout his time with us he has met every deadline and completed every project with professionalism and an upbeat attitude.

Phil has excellent management and organizational skills. His department runs smoothly and his staff is consistently enthusiastic and involved in their work.

I heartedly recommend Phil Jones for a position within your company. If you require any further information please do not hesitate to call. I have listed both my business and personal home number for your convenience.

Sincerely,
Former Boss
ABC Hotels

And then hopefully, the person will add some special touches in order to 'shine up' the letter:

To Whom It May Concern:

It is with pleasure, but also regret, that I write this letter of recommendation for Phil Jones.

I am pleased to write this letter because I know Phil is going to be a tremendous asset to your organization. I regret that I have to write this letter because Phil has been a pleasure to work with over the past two years.

Phil has been a Convention Sales Manager for ABC Hotels for the past two years. Throughout his time with us he has been exemplary in every area of his employment. His resume speaks for itself. He has excelled in every area of his professional life.

Phil has set an example for others to follow in terms of handling the disappointment of a layoff. He has been upbeat and positive.

I congratulate you, in advance, for selecting a truly outstanding employee.

Please feel free to contact me at the numbers listed below should you have additional questions.

Sincerely,
Former Boss
Manager, ABC Hotels

Sample: Letter to Request Outcome of Interview

Normally at the end of an interview the potential employer will inform you of when the decision is going to be made. If they do not, it is perfectly appropriate to ask them yourself.

> *"Thank you for taking the time to speak with me today Mr. Boss. Could I ask when you might be making the final hiring decision?"*

The response was—"We are going to make a decision in two weeks." And it is three weeks later and you have not heard. How do you find out what is happening?

If you have waited an appropriate amount of time you have two choices. You may either call or write a letter. If you call you want to keep your conversation brief and to the point.

"Good morning. My name is Bob Smith and I interviewed with Mr. Boss last week for the position of sales manager. At that time I was informed that the decision would be made last week and I have not heard anything yet. Would it be possible for me to find out if the decision has been made?"

If you receive no information, then your next step is to write a letter. The letter can basically be the phone call in paper form.

Dear Mr. Boss,

I interviewed with you on Oct. 22, 2001 for the position of Sales Manager.

At the end of our meeting you anticipated the decision being made by Oct. 29. I was wondering if that decision had, in fact, been made?

I am excited about the possibility of becoming part of your sales team. I look forward to hearing from you!

Sincerely,
Bob Smith

If you do not receive a response within a week, you can certainly call again. However, at this point I would suspect the decision had been made and the employer has obviously chosen not to inform the other applicants that the position has been filled.

Chapter Summary

❑ Have a general letter written all Opportunity Lists.

❑ Have a basic letter written for all miscellaneous letters.

19 Common Mistakes and 17 Common Concerns

CHAPTER GOALS

◆ To recognize common job search and interviewing mistakes.

◆ To provide answers to common applicant concerns.

◆ To complete any unfinished work from Days 1 through 7.

Today all you have is some reading. You should be able to read, and digest, the information in this chapter in a couple of hours. Use the rest of the day to complete company research or finish writing your Opportunity List letters or resume.

19 Common Mistakes

These are the mistakes most commonly made during a job search and interview. Eliminate these and your opportunities increase dramatically!

Not listening

Several years ago I met a professional interviewer at a friend's barbecue. When she learned the nature of my business, she began to talk about some of the problems she encountered on a daily basis. "I interviewed a very able gentleman today. He had great answers," she smiled. "Unfortunately his answers had nothing to do with the questions I was asking!" Hmm, I thought, a classic poor listener.

Too many people think they know what the question is going to be just by hearing the first few words of the sentence. Instead of paying attention to the whole question they quit listening and begin to plan their answer.

There will be subtle differences in questions that could cause you to answer incorrectly if you are not listening carefully. "Tell me about a company policy that you didn't agree with," could elicit a different response than, "Tell me about a company policy that didn't agree with and were able to change."

For these reason you must listen carefully to each question. Do not lag behind the interviewer by worrying that you just said something wrong. Do not get ahead of the interviewer by anticipating questions. Use the tactic LRDR:

- ◆ Listen (to the entire question).
- ◆ Replay (the question in your mind).
- ◆ Decide (on an appropriate response).
- ◆ Respond (using an appropriate story).

Thoughtful silence will not cause the interviewer any concern, especially if your response actually answers the question.

Trying to Lead the Interview

Although you do have a great deal of control over the information you provide, it is the interviewer who should choose the topic of conversation and lead the discussion.

I had one client who was told he did not get a certain job because he was not a good listener. When we first sat down to discuss this feedback, he had no idea what he had done to give this impression. We finally realized that he had been so nervous that the minute he met the interviewer he started talking. In his attempt to appear friendly, he had appeared frantic and overbearing. His non-stop talking gave the impression he was trying to lead the interview.

It is important to be friendly, but follow the lead of the interviewer. If they make small talk, of course you should join the conversation. If there is no small talk, don't talk just to break the silence.

Venting Personal Frustrations

Although you are in the interview to talk about yourself, now is not the time to explain how things *should* have gone in your life. It is not that interviewers are unsympathetic, but we have all had our share of hard times. The purpose of the interview is for you to give information, not gather sympathy.

Although you do not want to dwell on difficult situations, do not go overboard and try to make your life appear as though you have never encountered difficult decisions, problems, or conflicts. This type of presentation is unrealistic and unbelievable.

It is important to leave the interviewer with the impressions that, "Yes, it was difficult time/terrible situation. This is how I handled myself and what I learned from the situation. But, that is behind me and I am looking forward to new challenges."

Speaking Poorly of Others

If you speak ill of a past employer, co-worker, etc., the interviewer will immediately suspect that you may also speak poorly of him some day.

Not Being Professional

All the people you come in contact with are professionals within their field. Any hint of rudeness on your part will not be tolerated. In addition, this is not the time to look for favors or to ask for special treatment.

I heard about one applicant who, while sitting in the waiting room, interrupted a busy secretary and asked for more sugar for his coffee. (Gee, I wonder if he got hired?)

Also it is never, under any circumstances, appropriate to use profanity. (Even if you are relating a story and someone else said it—never use profanity!)

Losing Your Focus

It seems every industry is a small, close-knit community. It is not uncommon to bump into a friend or acquaintance in the company's offices while you are waiting for your interview. It is easy to slip into unsuitable conversations. Be careful of reminiscing, gossiping about other people, or bemoaning the state of the job market.

Once again, always remember where you are (at a competitive interview) and why you are there (to get a great job). Do not let outside circumstances allow you to lose your focus.

Not Sharing Your Attention

If two or more people are interviewing you, make sure you acknowledge them all. A good rule of thumb is to give the person who asked the question sixty percent of the eye contact, the silent person forty percent.

A common situation is to be interviewed by a man and a woman. People are still making the mistake of giving the man more of their attention. Not only is this rude, it does not say much for the applicant's communication and team orientation skills.

I learned this lesson from personal experience. I was making a presentation to a man and a woman and, unknowingly, directed ninety percent of my attention to the man. (How did I learn the woman felt slighted? She was my sister-in-law. Oops!)

Being Too Aggressive

It is true that you must be assertive in your job search. But beware! You must be careful that you don't become a pest.

Of course you should keep the potential employer informed of your continuing interest. A letter every four to six weeks will be enough to let any potential employer know that you are interested and available. But do not continually phone or drop by without an invitation.

I met an individual who called a company every week and dropped by to talk to anyone who would listen. After three months of this behavior the personnel director called him—not to invite him for an interview, but to let him know his behavior was disruptive and irritating.

Once you have made initial contact (the correct person has your resume and knows you are looking for a specific position or after you have had an interview) use the mail to ask for information or to update them on your activities. Do not call unless you are asked. Do not stop by unless you are invited. (Note: It is fine to call if you have not heard from the company concerning the outcome of a specific interview.)

Being Late

Don't be!

Have specific directions to the office. Check the weather for the day of the interview and plan accordingly. Plan on arriving at the interview site at least twenty minutes early. Then, sit in your car and spend a few quiet moments taking some deep breaths and getting excited about the upcoming opportunity.

Believing Your Experience Will Get You the Job

No one owes you a job. You can have the best technical background in the world but, if you come across as arrogant they will hire someone else.

Making a Decision Too Soon

Some people approach certain interviews with the thought, "I don't really want to work for this company, but I'll go for the interview experience." Then, during the interview, they realize the job is a better opportunity than they had anticipated.

It is very difficult to make up for a lack of enthusiasm. It does not make a positive impression to begin showing interest halfway through your interview. You never know what facts you will discover about a company and a position until you have done all the research and have had an interview. For these reasons you must never decide before an interview whether you want the job or not. Approach each interview with the goal of, "I am going to get a job offer!" Make your final decision only after you have all the facts.

Believing in Cycles

"No one hires during the holidays." "Everyone is on vacation during July." Employers are *always* on the lookout for good employees. In fact, your resume might be noticed quicker or your phone call may be returned faster during these perceived "down times" because other (less knowledgeable) job seekers have put their search on hold. Never stop your job search, or wait to start your job search because of holidays or vacation times.

Joking

I have a hard time telling a joke even when I'm completely relaxed. Personally, I have met very few people who can carry off a joke under the stress of an interview. Never plan to tell a joke or try to lighten up the interview.

> **Never plan on telling a joke in an interview.**

I had one client, who, in the course of our work together, kept asking me if it was OK to joke about this or all right to interject a funny quote about that. My answer was continually, "No." When we debriefed his interview it was obvious that he continued to believe that trying to be funny would be a plus. He admitted to me that during his interview he was overcome with the desire to tell a joke, the joke fell flat, and the interviewer appeared mildly insulted. He was not hired. (I always suspected he tried more than one joke.)

This does not mean that you shouldn't show a sense of humor! If something funny is said (whether by the interviewer or, *accidentally*, by you), smile or laugh! Also, you want to appear approachable and friendly, so use your smile often.

Not Researching the Company

44% of employers mention lack of research as a common problem among job applicants (according to a poll conducted by Accountemps).

Having knowledge about a company is a signal that you are truly interested and motivated to work for that specific business. If you do not do the appropriate company research you may not be viewed as a serious applicant.

Not Having the Correct Paperwork

Companies ask for paperwork for specific reasons. If you do not come prepared when you are trying to place your best foot forward, what does that say about how prepared you will be on a daily basis?

Having Sloppy Paperwork

The people making the hiring decision look carefully at an applicant's paperwork. Poor paperwork presentation says, "This person does not care." Remember, your resume and cover letters are *you* on paper.

Before sending off any paperwork ask yourself: If I were looking at this paperwork for the first time how would I feel about the person who sent it? Is it neat? Is the grammar correct? Is the spelling correct? Is the typing neat? In the case of an application, have all the directions been followed? Have the questions been answered clearly and completely? Is the paperwork folded neatly into the envelope?

Have a friend review your entire package before sending it. After spending hours working on a resume or cover letter it is difficult to pick up even glaring errors.

Poor Physical Presentation

When you mention physical presentation people usually think of the way someone dresses. Although clothing plays a large part physical presentation also includes body language, eye contact, your health, and your grooming. Now is the time to take an honest look at your overall presentation (more on this in Day Nine).

Poor Technical Preparation

If you need to brush up on your technical skills; do it. If you need to reacquaint yourself with professional regulations; get the books out. If you will need to demonstrate your sales skills; do some role-playing selling the company product. If you will need to speak in front of a group; ask your friends over and give a talk.

When I was in college, I almost lost a great summer job working for the National Guard at the Pentagon because I had neglected to brush up on my typing. I asked (OK, begged) to come back and retake the test the next day. The interviewer took pity on me. I spent the whole night practicing and actually improved my score by fifty percent.

Take the time to honestly critique your technical skills. You can be the greatest person in the world but if you can't do the job you won't be hired.

17 Common Applicant Concerns

♦ **I am a nervous wreck prior to an interview.**

♦ **During an interview I am so nervous that I talk too much and too fast!**

Almost everyone gets nervous before an interview. But, I know that fact doesn't help much when *you* are the one experiencing dry-mouth!

Let me share with you some lessons I've learned to lower your heart rate and dry up those sweaty palms.

When I began Cage Consulting I realized (due to a nonexistent marketing budget) that one of the best marketing tools available to me was the free informational talk. I called several local trade schools and offered to speak on job search techniques and resume writing.

When I hung up the phone after confirming my very first speech for sixty court reporters, I panicked. I remember thinking, "Wait a minute. I've never done this before!" All of a sudden, visions of failure popped into my head. I saw myself fumbling with notes, losing my place, tripping while walking on stage—you get the picture.

After several minutes of watching this personal nightmare, I realized that I was taking the first step toward certain failure. It became clear to me that if I continued to allow myself to think these thoughts I was going to talk myself into disaster. So, I told myself, "No more!"

For the next two weeks, every time a moment of doubt would creep into my mind, I would stop what I was doing and replace the negative thoughts with positive pictures. Instead of seeing myself fumbling with my notes or tripping up the stage, I would visualize myself being a success.

I saw myself looking fabulous and delivering my speech with poise and confidence. I pictured myself writing on a blackboard with strong bold strokes. I saw my notes organized in front of me in perfect order. I was always smiling and saw lots of smiling faces staring back at me. I would view these scenarios until the negative thoughts diminished.

My speech was just as I envisioned it. My audience laughed when I expected them to, asked lots of terrific questions and seemed genuinely interested in the topic. The speech was successful.

Excessive nerves detracts from an interviewer's ability to gather information and dilutes whatever confidence you may have in yourself. If you don't exhibit confidence in yourself, how can the interviewer feel confident about hiring you?

So, starting today practice positive visualization!

Visualize Yourself

Handling the Interview in a Confident and Professional Manner.
See yourself meeting the interviewer, giving him a firm handshake. Notice that your hands are cool and dry. See yourself in the interview room, breathing normally, and sitting up straight in your chair.

Picture yourself thinking through questions before answering. When you see yourself speaking, notice that you are looking directly at the interviewer and speaking with a strong voice.

Notice that you have a comfortable, confident smile.

> Practice positive visualization.

Doing the Job in a Flawless Manner.
See yourself in your new office handling problems and making decisions. Visualize yourself smiling during the process and handling yourself in a calm and professional manner. See yourself talking with other employees and enjoying your work.

Taking Your Time.
It is a fact of life that mistakes are made when people speak or move too quickly. You say something hurtful to a friend in the heat of an argument. You get a ticket because you are late for an appointment. You embarrass yourself, and others, by telling an inappropriate joke. After you say a hasty, "OK," you realize you don't have time to run that errand for your next-door neighbor.

None of these problems would occur if we all just took an extra second to think about the consequences of our words and actions.

This is also true in an interview. If you take an extra second to organize your thoughts before giving an answer, you will be much less likely to make a mistake.

Interviewers will not notice the extra time you take if they are rewarded with a thoughtful answer. By taking that extra moment you will show yourself as an individual who thinks through their options before reacting.

I had a client who was technically exceptional in his field. He had lots of experience and knew his job well. His one drawback was he reacted to everything at the speed of light. He spoke out of turn and interrupted people, and made mistakes in his work because he was moving too quickly. He needed to learn to slow down.

I have rarely met anyone who couldn't benefit from slowing down a little. During your daily routine practice taking an extra second or two to react to routine situations. Do not lunge to answer the phone on the first ring. Don't try to beat the yellow light at the intersection. Don't jump from line to line in the grocery store hoping to save thirty seconds. When someone asks you a question, take a second to replay the question in your mind before answering. Become comfortable speaking and reacting with a slower rhythm.

Also, try to limit your caffeine intake. When we are under stress the last thing we need is more stimulation! Cut down on the coffee, tea, colas, and chocolate.

- **I am working full-time while conducting my job search. How do I get people to meet with me other than during business hours?**

This is a common situation. Most employers who are interviewing are willing to be flexible.

When setting appointments briefly mention that you are working.

> *As I am working full-time I would like to ask that we meet during my lunch hour or perhaps in the morning prior to the beginning of the workday?*

If a person can only meet with you during the day, perhaps a phone interview would be the best way to get everything done without jeopardizing your current job.

These days many people don't mind meeting for coffee early on Saturday mornings. It is not out of line to suggest this. When you ask make it clear you understand if this is intruding on their free time.

However, never forget, YOU are the one who must show flexibility. Do not expect others to reorganize their lives for your convenience!

- **Right before I walk into the interview, I notice an error on my resume. Should I bring this to the interviewer's attention?**

No, if it is an error in spelling or grammar (unless you are applying for an editorial or administrative type of position).

Yes, if the error makes a difference in dates of employment, level of education, etc.

- **Should I tell the interviewer that I have another job offer and I need to know the outcome of my interview as soon as possible?**

Many applicants assume that this type of statement shows that they are in high demand. On the contrary you may well be viewed as a bit pushy.

Tell the company only under these circumstances:

- ◆ They *ask* if you have other job offers.
- ◆ Your other job offer needs an answer immediately. In this case call the company and ask to speak to the interviewer or the person making the decision. Very briefly, tell this individual your situation and ask if it would be possible to discover how soon the decision might be made.

"Thank you for taking my call, Mr. Jones. I very much want to work for your firm. However, I have been offered a position with another company and they are asking for a decision from me in 24 hours. I was wondering if it would be possible to find out when you will make decision on who you are going to hire?"

Be prepared for them to say they are unable to give you that information. You will then have to make a decision based on the information that is available to you.

Never try to use another job offer as a bargaining tool.

- **I always worry that my resume will get lost in the mail.**

Alleviate this worry by enclosing a self-addressed stamped postcard. On the message side of the postcard type:

> MCD Company_____Resume Received_____(please fill in the date).
> Thank you for dropping this in the mail.
> Sincerely, John Smith

- **What if I do not have all the requested documentation by the day of the interview?**

In your paperwork packet include an addendum sheet that lists all missing documentation. You want to include this sheet so that anyone reviewing your paperwork will understand that you did not simply forget to include a requested document.

For example, if you are missing a recent letter of recommendation from a past employer the addendum could read like this:

> Addendum to Requested Documentation
> John Doe
> 123 Anywhere Street, Denver, Colorado 88202
> (303) 555-5555
> Letter of Recommendation has been requested, but not yet received.

If you have old documents (such as a old recommendation letter from the employer) offer that. It will at least give the interviewer some of the information needed to conduct the interview.

- **Is it acceptable to call the interviewer and employees that I meet by their first names?**

As a general rule, no.

Use formal titles of Ms., Mrs., or Mr. during the interview. Do not use first names unless *specifically requested* to do so.

- **When I am telling my stores can I use the real names of the people involved in the situation I am describing?**

No. Remember it is a small world. It would not be surprising if the interviewer knew the person you were talking about. It is also possible that the person could have an interview with the same company.

It is easy to replace a name with a title. "I had a conflict with my supervisor. This supervisor . . . ."

If you feel the story becomes awkward without a name, make up a generic name. Make it obvious that this is not the real person's name. "Yes, I had a conflict with a co-worker I'll call Bob."

- **What if I need to reschedule my interview?**

It is not a positive to begin a relationship by making more work for the potential employer! Only reschedule if it is a true emergency.

If you must reschedule, make sure you have the dates of your availability in front of you. Call the company as soon as possible. Be prepared for the possibility that the company will have no additional dates available. You will have to decide, right then on the phone, whether you will keep the original appointment or cancel the interview.

- **How do I present additional documentation that I feel is important when the company has not requested it?**

At the end of the interview say something such as, "I have several letters of recommendation that I believe you might find informative. May I leave these with you?"

If they say "no," at least they know you came prepared. If they say "yes," then congratulate yourself on your forethought!

Do not overwhelm the interviewer with paperwork. Choose three to five of your best letters of recommendation. After five they become a blur. Do not present copies of diplomas or certificates unless asked.

- **What happens if the interviewer asks a question (technical or personal) and I simply do not know the answer?**

Personal: There are some questions that simply cannot be answered with a "no."

If you were asked about a conflict with a supervisor, or a difficult technical problem you encountered at work to answer, "No, that has never happened to me" would be unbelievable!

However, there are specific questions that might solicit a true, "no" response such as, "Can you tell me about an argument you had with a manager that got out of control?" It is very possible that this has never happened to you. Proceed to describe why you have never found yourself in that type of situation (you talk about things before they get to that point, etc.).

Technical: If you don't know the answer to a specific technical question, but you do know where to find the answer, share that information with the interviewer.

> *"Well, I am not sure about the exact first step you would take to fix that particular type of equipment. However, I would begin my search by looking in the manufacturer's FIXITALL catalogue."*

- **My interview is going to be over breakfast/lunch/dinner. What type of food should I order?**
  - ◆ Cereal and juice are good choices for breakfast.
  - ◆ For lunch a fruit salad or pasta salad are good choices. Don't choose a garlicky or spicy salad dressing; the smell lingers. If the only choices are sandwiches, choose one that is not messy. Your goal is to order something that is easy to handle.
  - ◆ For dinner select something that is mid-priced (not the cheapest nor the most expensive). Once again choose something that is easy to handle (no ribs or spaghetti). Do not order additional side dishes or hor d'oeuvres.

Whether or not to order an alcoholic beverage is a concern for many people. If your host tries to insist, and you do not drink, do not feel pressured. Politely decline and order iced tea, a sparking water or soda. If your host insists, and you are not averse to drinking, then make sure you sip your drink slowly so you don't have more than one cocktail.

Meal Etiquette
- ◆ Wait to be directed to your seat. Do not sit down until your host is seated or until you are invited to take your seat.
- ◆ Put your napkin in your lap soon after you sit down at the table.
- ◆ Do not eat the bread and butter before the meal. During the meal place your roll/bread on your side plate. Break your bread into small pieces. Lightly butter each piece individually before eating.
- ◆ Do not overly salt and pepper your food. Do not ask for extra condiments. Remember your primary goal is to focus on the interview, not eat.
- ◆ Do not begin your meal until everyone has been served. Wait until your host takes the first bite.
- ◆ When you are finished with your meal place your knife and fork parallel and together on the plate.
- ◆ If you have a lemon or lime in your beverage, cover the fruit with your hand when squeezing it into your drink.
- ◆ Do not complain about or send back your food. Unless it is completely raw (and it's not supposed to be) grin and bear it.

- ◆ If there are other job applicants at the meal include them in your conversation.
- ◆ Always thank your host for the meal.

- **I hate having to talk about money. What do I say when they ask me about my salary requirements?**

Many job seekers do not do enough homework when it comes to the salary part of the interview.

Prior to an interview research the salary structure within your city. Make some phone calls to people who are currently doing the job you are pursuing. If you ask for the information in a broad way, you will be surprised how helpful people will be.

> *"Hello, Mr. Collins. My name is Matt Adams and I'm calling to ask your advice. I am currently interviewing for the same type of position you hold, although obviously at a different company. My problem is I am a bit nervous about the salary negotiations. If I were to briefly describe my experience could you help me to understand what range I should be looking for?"*

There are also websites on the Internet that offer salary ranges throughout the country for various professions. A good start would be www.salary.com.

Before stating a salary range be aware of what benefit package would be included: medical, dental, retirement, vacation, etc. Leave room for negotiation. Try to have them give you a number first.

> *"Well, Mr. Brown, I know my salary would include some type of benefit package that the company offers. Could you give me a basic idea of what that might be?"*

> Or, *"I am very interested in working for your company, what salary range were you planning on offering?"*

> Or a mixture of the two: *"I am very interested in working for your company; obviously benefits are a part of the salary package. Could you give me a basic idea what that package might entail?"*

If they insist you give them a number talk only in terms of a salary range. Do not give the absolute lowest number in your range. If you have discovered that the average salary for your experience level and geographical area of the country is $45,000, then give your range as $46,000 to $50,000, depending on the benefit package. Make it obvious that there is room for negotiation.

Do not make the mistake of asking for your absolute minimum—that's what you'll get.

- **What if the interviewer asks a completely inappropriate question? (Are you going to have children? Do you go to church? What political party do you belong to?)**

Is losing a job offer over an inappropriate question worth it? That is a personal decision only you can make.

> **You must research salaries before negotiating.**

Personally, I would probably answer the question, unless it was lewd or disrespectful, and then decide later whether I wanted to work for this company.

- **What if I forget my interviewer's name?**

A trick to alleviate this problem is to listen carefully to the pronunciation of the name when you are first introduced. Then say the name immediately, "It is a pleasure to meet you, Ms. Franktown." Also, feel free to ask the name of the interviewer when your interview date is being arranged.

- **A company that is actively hiring has had my resume for over three weeks. I want to call and find out what is happening with my application. How should I do that?**

Take out your tracking sheet and refresh your memory as to what you sent the company and when it was sent. Then write out a script for your phone call. You want to appear organized and professional.

> Company Receptionist: *"Good morning, ABC Company, how may I help you?"*

> You: *"Good morning. My name is Samantha Evans. I am calling for Ms. Brown"* (the person who has your application).

Now, you will either be put through to Ms. Brown, or the receptionist will say:

> Company Receptionist: *"What is this concerning?"*

> You: *"Ms. Brown reviewed my qualifications for a position with your company. I am calling to follow up on her review."*

At this point the receptionist with either put you through or tell you Ms. Brown is unavailable. If she is unavailable ask for Ms. Brown's voice mail.

> You (Voice Mail Message): *"Good morning Ms. Brown. My name is Samantha Evans and I applied for the position of Office Manager. You received my resume on Oct. 12. The reason for my call is to follow up with you about when interviews might be taking place. My phone number is 555-123-4567. Thank you for your time. I look forward to hearing from you!"*

If you get to speak directly to Ms. Brown you can use the exact script as the voice mail message.

- **What should I take to my interview?**
  - ◆ Additional copies of your resume and application.
  - ◆ Documentation requested by the company.
  - ◆ Reference lists and letters of recommendation.
  - ◆ Pens and pencils.
  - ◆ A nice briefcase or folder to carry your documentation.
  - ◆ A light snack if your interview will take all day.
  - ◆ A toothbrush or mouthwash to use after a meal (in the restroom).

Chapter Summary

❑ If you can become aware of the most common mistakes made during an interview you chances will improve!

Physical Presentation

CHAPTER GOALS
* To organize your interview clothing.
* To practice your new skills by conducting a mock interview.

In another of my favorite movies, *Working Girl*, Sigourney Weaver (the evil boss) tells Melanie Griffith (the executive wannabe), "If you wear the wrong clothes, they'll notice the clothes. If you wear the right clothes, they'll notice the woman."

Before discussing physical presentation it is important to remember that this book was not written to present what is fair or what is right. It was written to give a job applicant the opportunity to learn how to deal with the real-life situations encountered during a job search.

For right or wrong, it is human nature to pay close attention to first impressions. If part of you tends to minimize this statement think about this scenario:

You are at a party where you don't know any of the guests. Before approaching anyone, examine your thoughts. If we were honest we would admit that we seek out people who we think look smart, witty or attractive.

If we notice people who dress sloppily, had dirty hair, or reeked of cologne, we would probably not pursue conversations with these individuals. Even if we did end up chatting with one of these people it would, very likely, take a long time to get past our first impression.

The same thing can, and does, happen in an interview. First impressions may be poor because an applicant is dressed inappropriately, her hair is messy, or he is embarrassingly disorganized.

Now is the time to take an honest look at the kind of overall impression you make. Ask yourself, and a trusted friend, these questions:

* Do I give the appearance of being in good health?
* Is my hair cut stylishly and neatly?

◆ Are my hands and fingernails neat and clean?
◆ Does my interview outfit fit me perfectly?
◆ Are my shoes appropriate?
◆ Do I wear too much jewelry? Do I wear too much cologne?
◆ (Women) Do I wear too much/too little makeup?

The clothing you wear to an interview will depend on the type of position you are applying for. Obviously it is impossible to discuss all types of situations, so I will offer some General Rules for Dress.

Men—General Rules for Dress

◆ Men are expected to wear a business suit to an interview.

- If the company is conservative it is best to wear a dark suit, starched (white or muted color) shirt, conservative tie, black shoes and socks.
- If the company or the position you are applying for is more liberal, clothing can be more liberal. Stick with a dark business suit. However, colored shirts, more colorful ties, suspenders, etc. will be much more acceptable.
- Even if the company allows casual dress on a daily basis, you should still wear a suit to the interview. This is a business meeting. For business meetings you dress in business attire.
- Try on your interview suit a few weeks prior to the interview. Make sure it fits well, is clean, pressed, and has no loose threads. Do not make the mistake of thinking, "Oh, they'll never notice the pants are a bit too short or the jacket sleeves are frayed." The interviewer will notice.

◆ Your shoes should be in good condition and polished. Make sure they don't squeak.
◆ Wear tall socks so that bare leg will not show when you are seated.
◆ Have your hair cut no more than three days prior to the interview.
◆ Make sure your nails are clean and groomed.
◆ Make sure your facial hair is neat. Pay special attention to stray hairs (nose, ears, eyebrows).
◆ Keep jewelry to a minimum. A watch, wedding or class ring, and tie clip are acceptable.
◆ Do not wear cologne. You never know who may have allergies.
◆ Make sure your briefcase is in good condition. Do not carry bulky canvas bags or backpacks.

Women—General Rules for Dress

◆ Although pants are now acceptable in the workplace, your interview suit should be much more formal. This means wearing a business suit with either a *matching* skirt and jacket or pants and a jacket.

Choose the color based on what type of position you are pursuing. For conservative businesses (accounting, law, medicine, etc.) it is best to keep your colors basic (black, navy, gray, brown, olive). However, make sure you choose a color that enhances your appearance. If you are uncertain as to what style or color fits you best take a trip to a better women's clothing store and ask a salesperson for assistance. Tell them the type of job you are pursuing and ask them to pick out suits for you to try.

If you are in a business that is more liberal (advertising, retail, art gallery) then you can select from a wider range of colors and styles.

◆ Although you want the length of your skirt to be fashionable, it is a good rule of thumb not to have the hem ride up more than two inches above the knee when you sit down.

◆ Make sure your shoes fit the occasion.

  • As a general rule heels should be no more than $1^1/_2$ inches. Anything higher and you may tend to wobble.
  • Do not wear open-toed or sling-back shoes. Do not wear shoes that have bangles, rhinestones, etc. as decorations. Choose a color that complements your clothing.

◆ Make sure the hose you wear matches your outfit. Do not make the mistake of wearing dark hose with a light colored suit or vice versa. When in doubt stay with neutral colored hose.

◆ Stay away from tight skirts. They are difficult to move in and many people find them inappropriate for the workplace.

◆ Stay away from linen. It wrinkles easily.

◆ You do not have to have a different outfit to wear for multiple interviews. It is much easier to change the look of a suit simply by wearing a different blouse or adding a scarf.

◆ Do not wear cologne. You never know who may be allergic.

◆ Make sure your nails are well groomed. Colored nail polish is fine as long as the color will be appropriate for the work atmosphere. (You wouldn't want to wear green sparkly nail polish if you were interviewing as a paralegal for a conservative law firm.)

- If you are unsure how to apply your makeup, invest in a makeup lesson.
- The jewelry you wear should complement your outfit. Simple, understated jewelry is always a safe bet (pearl or gold earrings, a simple necklace or pin on your jacket if appropriate, a watch, and wedding or class ring). Dangle bracelets will rattle. Earrings that are too big and heavy may be a distraction.
- If you carry a briefcase, do not carry a purse. Carrying more than one case can make you appear awkward.
- Keep an extra pair of pantyhose with you.

Men and Women
Handshake

A limp handshake accompanied by poor eye contact does not make a good first impression. It is better to have a handshake that is a little too firm rather than too relaxed.

Here are some tips for a professional handshake. These tips are applicable whether you are meeting a man or a woman.

- Don't be afraid to extend your hand first.
- Make eye contact the whole time you are being introduced.
- Smile!
- Take the person's whole hand in yours. Make sure your thumb is aligned with the other person's wrist.
- Make sure you can feel the other person's whole hand. If you are touching all the pressure points, the handshake should feel firm without crushing bones.
- Hold the handshake for as long as it takes to say, "It's a pleasure to meet you." Then release.

Sweaty hands

While you are waiting, keep your hands unclenched and let the air circulate around them.

Right before you meet someone, press the palm against your pants leg or skirt. The material will absorb a little bit of the excess moisture. Your hand may still be moist, but not dripping wet.

Smoking

Do not smoke, or be around smoke, in your interview clothing. Do not smoke the day of the interview.

I met with a client who smelled strongly of cigarette smoke. Being a non-smoker, by the end of our session together I had quite a headache. I suggested to him that he needed to have his suit dry-cleaned and mentioned he should not smoke around his interview clothing and paperwork. He looked surprised and said, "I don't smoke." It turned out his wife smoked. Even though they thought they had been careful by keeping his clothing and paperwork in the guest room, the cigarette smell was still very strong.

Mock Interviews

Now it is time to pull all your newfound knowledge together and take it for a practice spin.

A videotaped mock interview is one of the most important and beneficial preparation processes. You will learn more about how you come across to others from watching a half-hour video of yourself than you could ever learn in three weeks of constant critique from others. Watching yourself on videotape allows you to take a "third party" look at yourself. You will clearly see your mistakes and the things you do well!

Conducting a Mock Interview

The Mock Interviewer
Pick someone familiar with your industry and whom you trust to give honest feedback.

Dress
Set the stage to mirror the interview atmosphere. Wearing business attire will allow you to feel like you are in an interview.

Body Language
Make sure you sit calmly in your chair. Keep your bottom up against the back of the chair with your feet flat on the ground. Do not cross your legs.

Stage
Sit in a straight-back chair. Have the interviewer sit next to the camera. You should be the only person on camera.

Eye contact
When the interviewer is talking you should be looking at him, when you are talking you should be looking at him. However, when you need to think you may look away. Choose a "thinking spot" on the horizon (a wall switch, picture, etc.).

Camera View

Be careful of the lighting of the room. Make sure you have the light straight ahead of you. Do not have a lamp in back of you or to the side, as this will place your face in shadow. Have your interviewer sit to the side of the camera. You should always be looking at the interviewer, not the camera.

The camera should give a clear view of you from the knees up. You want to be able to view your entire body stance.

Questions

The interviewer should select the questions at random from the Self-Evaluation Questions. Also, provide your interviewer with a copy of your resume to help simulate more specific questions concerning your particular background. The mock interview should be at least $\frac{1}{2}$ hour long and include questions from all categories listed in the Self-Evaluation Worksheet.

Review

After the mock interview, ask your interviewer for initial reactions. Discuss how you felt and where you sensed you did well or not so well. Do your critiques match? If not, pay special attention to the areas of disagreement and perhaps get a third opinion.

It is important to remember that you must be open to constructive criticism. Do not get angry with your mock interviewer for giving his opinion. You asked for it! If you feel it is exceptionally harsh critique, ask someone else to do another mock interview to get a second opinion.

After your initial discussion, review the tape together. Stop the tape whenever you see a problem and discuss ways to improve.

Although this is a necessary and helpful exercise, it is important not to overdo it. Conducting numerous mock interviews will only cause you to become unrealistic in your critique. You will begin to look for perfection, which is impossible for any of us. Do no more than two mock interviews prior to a specific interview.

Chapter Summary

❑ Organize your interview clothes.

❑ Practice positive visualization.

❑ Complete, and critique, at least one $\frac{1}{2}$ hour mock interview.

DAY TEN
Implement Your Plan

Wow! You've done a lot of work in 9 days!

- Your workspace is set up for comfort and privacy. Your desk is supplied with paper, stamps, envelopes, business cards, and letterhead.
- You have a good start on a list of companies you wish to pursue.
- You have some basic research completed on companies of interest.
- Your Opportunity List letters are written and you have addresses for everyone on your lists.
- You have a basic resume that you can personalize easily depending on the situation.
- You have the beginnings of a comprehensive list of Networking Groups and Opportunities you are going to pursue.
- You have practiced your interviewing skills.

Now it is time to sew the seeds of your hard work and begin letting the world know you are available. After all this hard work and preparation I don't want you to lose your momentum.

Day Ten Activities

At the end of Day Ten the following tasks should be completed:

- All Friends/Relatives Opportunity List letters mailed.
- Initial cover letters and resumes sent to at least four companies of interest.
- You have selected at least two networking meetings you will attend within the next week.
- You have decided on a set time to review daily newspaper/ Internet job postings.
- You have begun the process of mailing your Business Acquaintance and Informational Interviewing Letters. All these letters should be out within one week.

As you go out "on your own" let me encourage you to take a few moments every evening to write down your plan-of-action for the next day. You must dedicate yourself to sticking to this plan!

Example
Daily Plan-of-Action
If you are able to work on your job search full-time.

List your morning ritual. Assign a specific time to report to your workspace.

6:30 AM .... Rise and Shine.

6:30-7:00 AM .... Exercise.

7:00-8:15 AM .... Shower, dress, drive kids to school.

8:30 AM .... Breakfast.

9:00 AM .... Report to workspace.
Send out four resumes to companies of interest.

9:30 AM to 10:30 AM .... Check specific company websites for job openings; check appropriate Internet job search websites. Begin research on four new companies. Begin follow-up on 2 resumes sent out 10 days ago.

11:00 AM .... Informational Interview with Mr. Brown.

12:30 PM .... Lunch at Professional Businessperson's Group.

2:00 PM .... Finish following-up on resumes. Organize business cards and jot down notes on people met at Professional Businessperson's lunch.

3:00 PM .... Make phone calls to 4 people on Opportunity List to discover if anyone has suggestions on job search.

4:30 PM .... Complete 'to do' list for tomorrow.

5:00 PM .... Congratulate myself for a job well done!

> Schedule your day and stick to your schedule.

Example
Daily Plan-of-Action
If you work during the day.

In order to complete the required daily tasks you may have to set your alarm clock for (at least) one hour earlier than normal.

5:45 AM .... Rise and Shine.

6:00 AM .... Shower, Dress.

6:30 AM .... Send out 4 resumes or applications to companies of interest.

7:00 AM .... Review newspaper/Internet job listings. Make a list of possible opportunities while eating breakfast.

Lunch hour .... Make follow-up phone calls to companies of interest and/or call people on Opportunity Lists to follow up on suggestions and advice. Or perhaps conduct a twenty-minute informational interview over the telephone.

6:00 PM .... Arrive home. Exercise, eat dinner. Spend time with family.

8:00 PM .... Company research. Send out three new resumes.

Or

6:00 PM .... Attend networking meeting.

7:30 PM .... Arrive home. Eat dinner. Spend time with family or exercise

9:00 PM .... Organize business cards and jot down notes about people you met at networking meeting. Review opportunities that need to be followed up on. Do company research. Write your Plan of Action for tomorrow.

10:30 PM .... Celebrate all your hard work by going to bed!

A Final Comment

One of the most important lessons I try to teach my clients is to learn from their mistakes. However, you can't correct mistakes unless you remember what they were.

It is imperative that you write down your impressions immediately after your interviews. Jot down specifics such as the names of the interviewers and their positions and the names of other employees you met. List the questions you were asked, and critique how you answered these questions. If you were dissatisfied with an answer, write down what you wish you had said. If you said something wonderful, write it down and preserve it for posterity—and to use at another interview.

Although no one wants to think about a negative outcome, if you are not offered a position you covet a courteous letter to the interviewer asking for feedback is not out of line.

> Dear Mr. Interviewer:
>
> Although I was disappointed to receive the letter informing me that the position of Customer Relations Manager had been filled, I do appreciate you giving me the opportunity to interview.
>
> I would like to be considered for other positions as they become available. Also, in order to improve my job search and interviewing skills I would appreciate your feedback on my interview and experience. I realize your comments may be general in nature. However, any feedback would be helpful.
>
> Thank you for your time.
>
> Sincerely,
> Your Name

Enclose a self-addressed-stamped envelope for his reply. If you do not hear anything take that as a sign that he cannot, or is unwilling, to give you any feedback. At this point do not pursue the matter further.

Do not call and ask for feedback. Ask by mail only.

Life is a continuing learning process. You *will* be successful if you remain persistent and strive to learn something new about yourself or the job search process on a daily basis.

And finally, do not lose hope. A job search is temporary. But, how temporary depends on your organization, your attitude, and your motivation to succeed. The good news is that all those things are within your control.

I wish you the very best. Let me hear from you!

Cheryl A. Cage
Tucson, Arizona
cheryl@cageconsulting.com

Pat yourself on the back for a job well done!

Before, During, and After Checklist

Before Applying

- ❑ Research the company.
- ❑ Request permission from past employers/co-workers/friends to use them as references.
- ❑ Prepare your resume and cover letters.
- ❑ Begin your study/practice for the technical and personal part of the interview.
- ❑ Prepare your interview clothing.

Before the Interview

- ❑ Organize your interview packet. Have on hand:
    - Additional copies of your resume and application.
    - Documentation requested by the company.
    - Reference lists and letters of recommendation.
    - Pens and pencils.
    - A nice briefcase or folder to carry your documentation.
    - A light snack if your interview will take all day.
    - A toothbrush or mouthwash to use after a meal.
- ❑ Pay close attention to grooming details.
- ❑ Know the route to the interview site.
- ❑ If possible, visit the site prior to your interview. If you must travel to another city for your interview, do not go at the last minute. You will be much more comfortable if you give yourself at least a day to settle in. Also, stay at a hotel close to the site of the interview. If you have friends in the city where your interview is taking place, resist the temptation to visit late into the evening prior to the day of your interview. Give yourself some "alone" time to focus and prepare for the next day.
- ❑ Do not drink any alcoholic beverages for at least two days prior to the interview. Alcohol can affect you differently during times of excitement or stress.
- ❑ Do not smoke around your interview clothing. Do not smoke the day of the interview.

Day of the Interview

❑ Be in your "interview mode" no matter what circumstances you find yourself in (sitting in the waiting room, filling out paperwork, eating lunch between interviews).

❑ Plan to arrive at the interview site at least half an hour before the interview. However, do not arrive at the interview more than 15 minutes early.

During the Interview

❑ Pay close attention to the pronunciation of the interviewer's name and any employees you may meet.

❑ Listen to the questions.

❑ Be polite, friendly and focused on giving the most specific, concise answers possible.

❑ Be positive and enthusiastic about possible employment.

❑ Maintain good eye contact.

❑ Smile!

After the Interview

❑ If you are unsure as to the address and correct spelling of the interviewer's name, ask the receptionist on your way out.

❑ Write down specific questions that you felt you answered well—or not so well. Describe your overall impressions.

❑ Write the interviewer a brief thank you note. The note can be handwritten (if you have nice handwriting) on a plain white note card. Or, you may type a note on the same type of paper as your resume. The note does not have to be longer than two short paragraphs.

- Thank him for his time.
  Thank you for speaking with me last Thursday.
- Show enthusiasm towards employment.
  I am excited about the opportunity to become a part of your growing company.
- End by leaving the door open to contact him again.
  I hope that we have the opportunity to speak again soon.

APPENDIX I
Information Resources

At the time of publication telephone numbers and website addresses were checked for accuracy. However, we cannot guarantee that the information provided on these websites is correct, or that the offers made are valid.

Job Search Sites

I list these sites not because I believe the Internet is where you will uncover your job. A very small percentage of people (I have read less than 4%) receive a job offer through an Internet job search.

I list these because I *do believe* the Internet is an excellent tool to use for company and career research. Some websites offer Chat Rooms where you can post a question to professionals in your field to learn more about the career field and job opportunities within certain areas of the country. Some websites offer both national and international job opportunities.

America's Job Bank www.ajb.dni.us	Partnership between U.S. Dept. of Labor and State Public Employment Services. Access 1M jobs on line. Post resume, job search and job-seeking services.
Career Magazine www.careermag.com	Search for jobs; informative articles on interviewing, resume writing, relocation services.
Career Mosaic www.careermosaic.com	Headhunter.net. Resume postings, resource center.
Career City www.careercity.com	Concentrates on health care, government, education, pharmaceutical jobs.
Career Web www.careerweb.com	Career advice, post resume, search jobs.

Appendix I

Guru www.guru.com	General career opportunities. Must register to use this site.
Management Jobs www.managementjobs.com	Executive search board. Positions start at $50,000 and up. Job search workshops nationwide.
www.Monster.com	General job database.
Virtual Job Fair www.vjf.com	High tech job listings. Job fair schedule by locale.

Private Industry Resources

Many companies post job openings on the company website. Many also have job hotlines that are updated weekly.

Go to a search engine such as Google.com or Yahoo.com and search under the company name. For example, during our research we searched in Google.com under :

- ◆ Flight Safety International
- ◆ Raytheon
- ◆ IBM

We first discovered the main 'Home Page' for each company. From there we researched job opportunities. (Do not be discouraged if the Job Openings page comes up at 'this page cannot be displayed.' Many times companies are updating these sites. If you continue to receive the 'this page cannot be displaced' message search the website for a phone number to call for information.)

Some companies also have info on their site that discusses the various Business Areas within their specific company. This type of information will help you decide if any of your talents would fit into the company.

120

Local and Federal Resources

Local municipalities, state government and federal agencies also provide on-line access to job listings.

Examples of Federal Listings

U.S. Dept. of Labor & Employment   Federal agency.
www.doleta.gov

Federal Jobs Central   Job site for federal positions/
www.fedjobs.com   pay/training

Federal Aviation Administration   Jobs within the FAA
www.faa.gov

Some Examples of State Listings

We used Google.com and searched under State of California and received links to civil service jobs and employment. Under State of Georgia we received a link to the State of George Department of Labor.

As another example here are a listing of department titles for the State of Colorado. Use these examples of department titles to begin research on similar programs within your state.

Many *counties* also have job centers. Do NOT be discouraged if the types of jobs are non-professional, lower wage. Remember this is only one place to do research!

Example: State of Colorado

Arapahoe County Jobs   County by county Job Service
www.arapahoeco.us   Centers.

Colorado Workforce Centers   Associated with Dept. of
http://employsvcs.cdle.stateco.us   Unemployment and Training

So, if you live in Iowa look for Iowa Workforce Centers. Also look within individual *cities* for assistance programs or retraining programs.

City and County of Denver   Dislocated worker tuition
www.denvergov.org   programs, workshops, skills
          building, job search seminars.

Colorado Jobs   Listings of jobs available in
www.coloradojobs.com   the State of Colorado

Starting Your Own Business

When you dislike your work, or are having trouble finding a position within your field many people dream about starting their own business. At first glance this may appear to be a more attractive option than working for someone else. However, unless you have been researching and thinking about a business for a long time, now is probably not the best time to invest a lot of time and money into your own business.

That doesn't mean that having your own business isn't a good option. However, my advice would be to secure meaningful employment first, then take your time developing a solid business plan. Taking this approach will allow you to have a steady income while you develop a realistic business start-up plan.

A good starting point for information on starting a business, buying a business, or financing a business is the Small Business Administration website at www.sba.gov. Also by using a search engine such as Google.com and typing in 'starting your own business' you will find several good sites for beginning business owners.

Skills Assessment

We are all multi-talented. Sometimes we just don't know it until we are forced to do some research into ourselves.

Uncertain as to Your Career Options?

To find your true career-niche, it is imperative that you muster up all of your creative energy. You need to be able to accept the fact that change will occur only with some hard work and thought on your part. The sooner you accept that reality the quicker you will take control of your job situation.

As you work through the Skills Assessment Exercises don't dismiss any idea immediately. Let all the ideas you come up with, or ideas that others offer to you, simmer for a while.

I saw a story on television about a woman who, at the age of 50 or so, was told by her doctor that within six months she might lose most of her sight.

She went into a deep depression. She had always talked about wanting to learn to paint so her husband, in an effort to lift her spirits, bought her some paints and canvas and told her to do something even if it was a bad painting.

Slowly, she discovered she had talent. In fact, it turned out she had remarkable talent as an artist. Her desire to continue painting was so strong she figured out a way to "feel" the color of paint by working with the various temperatures of the paint color. Even with her limited sight she has sold several of her paintings and is making a name for herself in the art world. Out of a terrible hardship she discovered a passion in her life.

You also have hidden talents. You need to take the time and put in the effort to discover what talents are dormant within you. What skills do you have that could translate into work?

As you work through these exercises, do so with a feeling of anticipation. Who knows? You might be at the beginning of a journey towards discovering a hidden passion or a valuable talent.

Have a Career Choice but Want to Develop Other Talents?

Perhaps you are confident as to your main career path, but you have taken to heart my suggestion of developing more than one marketable talent. Good for you! Just have fun with the following worksheets. Don't dismiss any idea immediately. Let all the ideas you come up with, or ideas that others offer to you, simmer for a while. You may be well on your way to discovering a hobby or talent that could translate into a money making idea.

Basic industries

Before we begin with skills assessment, here is a basic list of industries where job opportunities exist. As you read through these lists of industries and job possibilities please realize that this is a minute listing of possibilities. My goal is to jump start your creative thinking. Make sure you share these exercises with a trusted friend or relative. The more people you brainstorm with the more ideas you will uncover.

Non-manufacturing
Agriculture/Forestry/Fishing/Energy/Mining/Construction

Manufacturing
Producing products in quantity

Transportation
Road/Water/Air/Communications/Utilities

Wholesale Trade
Sell products

Retail Trade
Sell products to the public

Finance
Banks/Insurance/Real Estate/Securities/Investments

Services
Lawyer/Non-Profit Organizations

Public Service
Government/Military/Politics/Taxation/Public Safety/Health

Education
Middle, High School, College Level/Tutor/Adult Education

Freelance
Business Owner/Tutor/Consultant (in any area)

Within these specific industries you usually have 8 basic skills in each area:

- Operations
- Finance
- Research and Development
- Sales and Marketing
- Human Resources
- Information Systems
- Legal
- Administration

As you go through the following Skills Assessment Brainstorming Exercises keep these industries and basic skills in the forefront of your mind. Your goal is to search for a match between your skills and the business community.

Skills Assessment Brainstorming: Exercise #1

What activities do you enjoy that allow you to forget about time? Is there an activity or hobby that you can begin at 9 in the morning, only to be completely surprised that it is now well past noon? Some possibilities:

Playing a sport.

Writing.

Playing a musical instrument.

Studying plants or gardening.

Working as a volunteer for a cause in which you believe.

Designing websites.

Searching the Internet.

Studying astronomy.

Working on computer programs.

Studying the weather.

Working on your financial portfolio or studying the stock market.

Researching your family genealogy.

Tutoring a child or working in adult education.

As you can see there are a wide variety of activities that different people enjoy. My goal in asking you this question is to get you thinking about what type of work could encompass talents you already enjoy. Let me give you some examples of what I mean:

- After I lost my job as a flight attendant I went to work in sales and marketing. I noticed my workday went by quickly when I had a marketing copy to write. I loved the writing process! I realized that I should pursue work that required a great deal more writing than I was doing.
- A friend of mine has always been passionate about politics. She volunteered for a campaign and had the time of her life, plus she discovered she had a knack for organization. A few months after her initial volunteer work she landed a paid position within a congressional campaign. After this campaign was over she was offered a part-time job with a small political research firm.
- Another friend is a passionate gardener. This passion has translated on several occasions into opportunities to assist with field studies. This passion could translate into various jobs that would offer a little extra money towards his retirement.

Now you answer the question: What type of activities do I enjoy that allow me to forget about time?

List at least three activities. When you are done, place your list aside and continue reading this chapter.

1. _____

2. _____

3. _____

Now, let's review my list again. But, this time, I have offered ideas for jobs that could grow out of these interests.

Playing a sport.
- Coach or manage intramural teams through your city government.
- Private coaching in your sport (tennis, ice skating, hockey, soccer, etc.).
- Personal Trainer at a health club or offer the service to individuals.

Writing.
- Freelance magazine writer.
- Speechwriter for executives or politicians (or those running for political office).

Playing a musical instrument.
- Play in local music clubs.
- Give music lessons.

Study plants or avid gardener.
- Work as a specialist in a nursery.
- Garden designer.
- Landscaper.
- Plant caretaker for businesses/office buildings.

Volunteer fundraiser or coordinator.
- Fundraiser for non-profits.
- Non-profit administrator.

Working on the computer.
- Computer trainer for individuals.
- Become a computer technician.

Designing websites.
- Consultant for a company that designs, or maintains, company websites.

Searching the Internet.
- Researcher for companies that provide specific research for companies and individuals.
- Teach people how to do research (on any topic) using the Internet.
- Researcher for authors writing non-fiction books.

Amateur astronomer.
- Work for a company that sells telescopes (retail, to the government and in the commercial sector).
- Lead stargazing workshops or teach young adult or adult classes in astronomy.
- Work in the area of meteorology.
- Teaching assistant at a community college.

Working on your financial portfolio or studying the stock market.
- Work as a consultant to a financial planning service.
- Research stocks for a financial information website.

Researching your family genealogy.
- Offer your research services to others interested in their family history.

Tutoring a child or adult.
- Offer your tutoring skills to parents of children needing extra assistance in school.
- Offer your skills through a community college.
- Work at a company that offers consulting in your area of expertise (i.e., computer tutors).

Ok, now pick up your list of three activities you enjoy. Get a cup of coffee or a cold drink and spend some time brainstorming about possible jobs that would match those talents. Do not dismiss any idea at first glance. Write every possibility down and allow the idea to simmer.

HINT: If you are having trouble thinking of specific types of industries or companies read the Yellow Pages.

Skills Assessment Brainstorming: Exercise #2

List 5 skills your family and friends compliment you on.

1. _____

2. _____

3. _____

4. _____

5. _____

Some possibilities:

Outstanding organizational skills.

Excellent drawing or painting skills.

Terrific graphic designer.

Great party planning skills.

Gourmet cook.

Excellent teaching skills.

Great with kids.

Knowledgeable about horses.

Good with animals.

Patient and excellent problem solver.

Gregarious and good public speaker.

Great with numbers.

Knowledgeable about computers.

Excellent carpentry skills.

Knowledgeable about antiques.

Don't go any further until you have listed 5 traits you are complimented on.

Now that you have your list, let's review my list. Once again I've listed jobs that could grow out of these types of innate skills.

Outstanding organizational skills.
- Administrative Assistant.
- Office Manager.
- Personal Assistant to business owner.
- Offer your organizational skills to numerous small business owners in your area.
- Home office organizer for individuals.

Excellent drawing or painting skills.
- Private art teacher to individuals or through adult education.
- Work for an interior decorator to complete mural paintings or faux painting for their clients.
- Illustrator for books.

Terrific graphic designer.
- Desktop publisher.
- Design book covers.
- Design marketing materials (brochures, letterhead, logos) for local businesses.

Great party planning skills.
- Work for a caterer or offer your services independently to companies or individuals (weddings, birthdays, office celebrations, etc.).
- Work in the catering department at a local hotel.

Gourmet cook.
- Chef.
- Provide cooking lessons at a local gourmet store.
- Work for a small catering company as chef or meal planner.

Excellent teaching skills.
- Tutor for your area of expertise.
- Adult education instructor.
- Develop a seminar based on your expertise.

Great with kids.
- Activities Director for After School Program through your local school district.
- Develop/ direct various programs for kids through non-profit organizations in your area.

Knowledgeable about horses.
- Give riding lessons.
- Train horses.
- Work at a riding stable or facility.

Good with animals.
- Pet sitting business.
- Offer pet obedience lessons.
- Get some specialized education and train security dogs, guide dogs, etc.

Patient and excellent problem solver.
- Work for a job search firm.
- Work for a credit-counseling firm.

Gregarious and good public speaker.
- Sales of products you believe in (retail or wholesale).
- Trainer within a corporation.
- Real estate.

Great with numbers.
- Accounting.
- Bookkeeper.
- Officer bookkeeping services for small businesses or individuals.
- Math tutor.
- Real estate appraiser.

Knowledgeable about computers.
- Computer programmer.
- Teach computer skills to individuals.

Excellent carpentry skills.
- Design and build custom cabinets, furniture.
- Design outdoor decks, gazebos, playgrounds.

Knowledgeable about antiques.
- Offer appraising for individuals.
- Lead antique shopping trips (within your city, state or even the world!).

The above questions require some thought! Take the time to seriously review your skills, your passions. Take the time to meet with your friends and family to ask them for their input.

With a little time and some thoughtful assessment, I know you can come up with at least three areas of job possibilities that appeal to you.

Cage Consulting Products and Services

To Review or Order Books or Ask Questions
Call Toll Free: 1-888-899-CAGE (2243) or Visit Our Website:
www.cageconsulting.com

Checklist for Success: A Pilot's Guide to the Successful Airline Interview
By Cheryl A. Cage
Over 20,000 copies sold. Updated Yearly.

Checklist CD: An Interview Simulator
By Cheryl Cage
Applicants answer questions in a correct/incorrect manner and Cheryl critiques. Also: paperwork, self-evaluation. (Companion to *Checklist* book.)

Airline Pilot Technical Interviews: A Study Guide
By Ronald McElroy
Approach plates, weather, AIM, FARs, mental math, cockpit situations to analyze.

Mental Math for Pilots
By Ronald McElroy
Mental math tips and tricks for interview and cockpit use.

Reporting Clear? A Pilot's Guide to Background Checks
By Cheryl Cage
Pre-employment background checks are an important part of the selection process. Do-it-yourself background check and reasons why you should conduct your own background check prior to filling out employment applications.

The Resilient Pilot: Pilot's Guide to Surviving, & Thriving, During Furlough
By Cheryl Cage
Real-world, motivational guidance to help find enjoyable work outside the cockpit.

Pilot E-TrainingTest: Mental Math
By McElroy/Cage
Gauge your mental math abilities then improve them with this online mental math study tool. To order this online study guide visit www.cageconsulting.com

Welcome Aboard! Your Career as a Flight Attendant
By Becky S. Bock (Cage)
A complete guide to understanding the job of F/A and preparing
for interviews.

Coming in 2002

Your Job Search Partner: A 10-Day, Step-by-Step, Opportunity Producing Job Search Guide
By Cheryl Cage

Calm in the Face of Conflict
Twelve Surprisingly Powerful Strategies for Handling Conflicts and
Misunderstandings.
By Cheryl Cage

Technical Flash Cards: FAR, AIM, Approach Plates, Weather, and More!
By Ronald McElroy

Notes

Notes

Notes

Notes

Notes

Notes